how not to
stay single
after 40

Also by Nita Tucker

How Not to Screw It Up:
10 Steps to an Extraordinary Relationship

How Not to Stay Single:
10 Steps to a Great Relationship

how not to
stay single
after 40

The Secret
to Finding Passion,
Love, and Fulfillment
—At Last

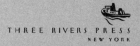

THREE RIVERS PRESS
NEW YORK

NITA TUCKER

Published by Three Rivers Press, New York, New York. Member of the
Crown Publishing Group.

Random House, Inc. New York, Toronto, London, Sydney, Auckland
www.randomhouse.com

THREE RIVERS PRESS and the Tugboat design are registered trademarks
of Random House, Inc.

Printed in the United States of America

Design by Susan Maksuta

Library of Congress Cataloging-in-Publication Data
Tucker, Nita.
How not to stay single after 40 : the secret to finding passion, love, and
fulfillment—at last! / by Nita Tucker.—1st ed.
p.   cm.
1. Middle aged women—Psychology.   2. Single women—Psychology.
3. Self-esteem in women.   4. Dating (Social customs)   5. Mate selection.
6. Man-woman relationships.   I. Title
HQ1059.4.T83   2002
305.244—dc21   2001045693

ISBN 0-609-80588-6

10 9 8 7 6 5 4 3 2 1

First Edition

To Debra Feinstein,

for finding the relationship of your life

after forty

acknowledgments

My thanks to:

Doug Preston: for your ongoing encouragement.

Ann Overton: Working with you is so easy and fun. You are a masterful writer.

Harvey Klinger: my agent, for believing in me.

Shaye Areheart: for always being supportive, excited, and my biggest fan.

My gorgeous, loving husband, Tony Tucker: for being just that—totally loving and gorgeous.

And a special thanks to the many ladies who shared their secrets with me, especially Dawn, Debra, Nan, Pat, Ann, and Sharon.

contents

how not to
stay single
after 40

introduction

This book is for women over the age of forty who want to find a loving, passionate, and nurturing relationship.

It is not about finding an adequate relationship, one that is "good enough for someone my age," but a stellar, better-than-your-dreams, awesome, "light-up-my-life" kind of relationship. It is about having a relationship that up to now was supposedly available only to the young or those who could afford the young.

If all this book covered were how to be attractive so you could find this true love (which it does!), then, of course, it would be worth taking your time to read it.

But what makes this book unique is that it is about what is available, what is possible, what is different, and what is better about a relationship at your age. Instead of trying to imitate or repeat what it was like to be in love like a couple of twenty-year-olds, how about the real thing of being in love like a couple of forty-five-year-olds?

Sound pretty depressing? How come? How come we think that everything great is either over or has passed us by? Is that really true? When I ask people what it is like to be the person they are now rather than who they were at twenty-five, without exception, everyone has said that they now have much more self-respect and self-esteem, are much happier with themselves, much more at peace, and definitely more nurtured by their relationships with others. So how could a relationship between two such evolved human beings not help but be better?

The answer is that we often throw away all these assets it took so many years to accumulate in order to try to relive or recapture some picture from the past. We do this because the only models we have for falling in love are from our (or others') youth. But looking and acting as if we are twenty when you are fifty doesn't work. You may have seen women who try to do this. Inevitably, the very attractive, beautiful, sensual, middle-aged woman will not only look like a fool, but the cover-up will actually make her look older than her age. The same thing happens when a relationship is forced into an inappropriate mold: its natural beauty becomes disfigured.

It Can Be Even Better with Age

My friend Martha, who just turned fifty, was telling me about the new man in her life. "Nita, what I am going through in this relationship I have never experienced before in my life." She was nervous and scared, just as she had been when she was young and in love, but her emotions and her way of relating to another human being were bringing forth a new discovery of herself. This makes a lot of sense. After all, we have grown and evolved as we grew older, so it is only natural that our relationships would expand and grow as well. I was truly excited by her news.

In interviewing women about what is better about relationships at our age, they always answered with what was better about themselves at this age. I kept going after what more they were getting out of the relationships, and still they kept telling me how much happier they were with themselves. Finally, I got it.

My advice about whether to continue dating a man or move on has always been to check how you feel about yourself when you are with him. If you feel admired, respected, listened to, and attractive when you are in his company, then keep going out with him. I realized that as we get older and feel better about who we are, we are more sure of who we are. As a result, we get more out of being with another person, and the other person's feelings about us get through more easily.

I interviewed many people for this book, both men and women. The results and insights from those conversations appear throughout the book. The men I talked with showed a bias for women over the age of forty, and they were, without exception, successful and accomplished men who could easily have courted and won women in their twenties and thirties. One of the questions I asked only the men was, "What do you like about women in this age group more than younger women?"

> *"I like to share a similar frame of reference with a woman. We have more in common and can talk about ideas from a similar background and period of time. Also, I find that younger women (and I was the same way when I was younger) are more theory and less experience. Younger people have all the answers and, interestingly, seem more closed-minded because of this."*

> *"I find that women my age have a better sense of humor. I seem to be on a different wavelength from the younger women I go out with. Also, I find a woman who has lived a little, who has had some ups and downs, more interesting and attractive."*

> *"If you want to have a certain quality of discourse and conversation, it requires a similar frame of reference. With younger women, I feel as if I am always in charge. There's no equality, because I am expected to mentor, mold, and direct. Some men like this, but personally, I find it exhausting."*

> *"I find older women are less into histrionics and drama and have a more developed sense of self. They tend to be more satisfied with who they are. I find maturity attractive. The calm and serenity of a woman who has taken care of herself both internally and externally are beautiful."*

"There's less time spent playing games and more time to just enjoy being together. I apologize for speaking of women as objects, but I compare an older woman to a ripe piece of fruit. When fruit isn't ripe, it's hard, not inviting, not vulnerable. When it's ripe, it's juicy, sweeter, softer, more giving, not so rigid."

Here are some observations from the women I interviewed about what they found better about relationships at this age:

"I am so much surer about who I am. I have so much more confidence and self-esteem, so I don't look to a man to give it to me. I can be myself. I am not constantly adjusting my thinking, my feelings, and my needs to accommodate the man I am with." (Without exception, every woman I talked with echoed this one point.)

"I know what I want, and I get it. I don't lower my standards, nor do I sacrifice my integrity for a man. Everything is much cleaner and clearer."

"I'm not on the emotional merry-go-round I was on when I was younger. I'm more calm and serene and therefore more present. I think I'm much more fun to be with, and I sure as hell know I have more fun."

"When I was younger, I felt I needed to please a man to keep him around and taking care of me. Now I can please a man

because I love him and want to. Sex is pure pleasure now rather than a means to an end."

"I'm not worried about making some terrible mistake that will ruin it all. I feel confident that I am bringing something to the relationship."

"I don't have to do significant, impressive things to convince myself I'm in a good relationship. I can have a wonderful day just being with my man watching old movies."

As older women, we also have more energy to "indulge" in a relationship than we did when we were younger. Though we may be busier, usually the energy that was required to prove ourselves in a career or as mothers has relaxed. Even men who tend to be strongly involved in their careers in their twenties and thirties are often more available when they are older. They have time to explore themselves with another person and are much more able to focus on what is possible in a relationship. Often they are motivated by their regret at not having been around and available when they were younger and now feel they missed out on seeing their children grow up.

In my own marriage, though I have more to juggle than ever with two children and a career, I feel more present and more able to dwell in the moment. I don't mean just during our times alone but in our everyday conversations, which are less about the business of living together and managing a family and more about the random thoughts, ideas, and other inner workings of the mind and soul.

Times Have Changed

Thirty or forty years ago, writing this book would have been thought as absurd as writing a "how-to" book for your home office. Of course, there were single women after forty but not enough of them to warrant a book.

Mostly, we felt sorry for them. Usually, the woman was single because she was a widow, something she was expected never to get over. "Poor Jane. She just lost her husband. She's just a shell of her former self." If the woman was divorced, no matter what the circumstances, she often fared worse. Perhaps she had cheated on her husband, had a drinking problem, or was simply a pitiful victim, stupid for having gotten involved with the jerk. And if she was the victim, she ought to look the part, because if she looked happy, confident, and attractive, then she had somehow brought it on herself. "Irreconcilable differences" did not exist as a legitimate reason for breaking up a marriage—whether in a courtroom or just among family and friends.

Someone who was neither divorced nor widowed was also suspect and perhaps an even greater mystery. The labels of *bachelor* and *spinster* were dreaded and shameful. You never knew exactly what it was, but certainly, something was very wrong. Either the person was a homosexual, then a horribly frightening curse to be hidden from everyone (why do you think "the closet" was conceived?) or mentally defective (when I was a child, my only unmarried relative was a cousin who was retarded) or probably the worst stigma, just plain unwanted.

In addition to classifying "older" people looking for a relationship as second-class citizens, there was an underlying feeling that love, romance, courtship, and marriage were open only to the young. Even married couples on television or in films were rarely shown as passionate toward each other.

The term *single* didn't really come into use until the late seventies. Before then, you were either a teenager, a student, or someone who was "dating." After age thirty, none of these "cute" terms applied, so you fell into the category of "un." You were unmarried, which implied unfinished and perhaps unwanted. This was something to be hidden; you were someone of whom to be wary; there definitely was little possibility of regarding the future with a positive outlook.

But, thank God, times have changed! Now more than 40 percent of the adult population is unmarried, and it is considered normal—and in many cases, even enviable—to be forty, fifty, or sixty and single. Unfortunately, however, the stigma of being single has survived and still is very much alive in small pockets of the population. This stigma is primarily concentrated in two locations—your parents and yourself. Your parents I can't deal with. I had a hard enough time dealing with my own. But in Chapter 2, I will talk about how *you* can eradicate this outdated, unproductive, and bothersome attitude.

My previous books all stemmed from my personal experience, enhanced with the experiences of others who have taken my seminars and classes. Because I was thirty-two when I met my husband, for this book I have relied on research and observation. I must admit I wasn't encouraged when I started out. In fact, at one point I told a close friend, "Here I am, almost fifty, and if something happened to Tony, how would I ever find a fabulous relationship? Any man I'd be interested in would want a thirty-year-old, and you know what? I wouldn't blame him."

Fortunately, from interviewing many women after forty who have found "the best ever" relationships, I have dug my way out of that deep, dark hole. For those of you who would like to do the same, sing hallelujah, this book is for you. I have uncovered their secret to finding true happiness for themselves, including when they are not in a relationship. This book gives you access to that secret and then gives you all the appropriate actions to take to find the relationship of your dreams. Many of these actions can also be found in my book *How Not to Stay Single*, but they have been revised and updated here to work for women after the age of forty.

the secret

Before I began writing this book, I knew all the reasons why it is more difficult for a woman after forty to find a relationship. Here are just a few of them:

Men want younger women and can get them.

Women's appearance sags and fades as we age.

Men want women they can mold.

Women are more set in their ways.

Men are more set in their ways.

All the good men are taken.

Men are intimidated by powerful, independent women.

Whatever the reason, the bottom line is inevitably the same: any man we would be interested in is either already taken or not interested in us.

Having worked for more than seventeen years helping both men and women find the relationships they want, I found it painful to witness the resignation I saw in women after forty about finding a really satisfying, fulfilling relationship. So I took on the mission of discovering what it would take for these women to overcome whatever obstacles they encountered and have the same kind of success a woman in her twenties or thirties could expect.

Fortunately, it didn't take me long to find plenty of women after forty or fifty who have found great relationships and to uncover their secrets. What do they know that others don't, and is it transferable?

Not surprisingly, none of the women I talked with advocated the conventional wisdom that, to find a man, you will have to curtail your power, your point of view, or your desires and interests. And while each of the women I talked with is physically attractive, none of them look like twenty-year-olds or like Sophia Loren—and some of them are not even thin.

Initially, I found that what all these women who have been successful in finding great relationships have in common are three very specific qualities. And the great news is that not only is it possible for any woman to cultivate or adopt these qualities, but the qualities are worthy, desirable, and admirable in and of themselves.

The three qualities every woman needs in order to find and keep a truly great relationship are:

1. A profound sense of yourself as a person you *genuinely* like, admire, and respect—in other words, a high level of self-esteem

2. Being fun—having fun in your life and being someone
   who is fun to be with
3. An authentic enjoyment of your own sexuality and sex,
   not as a way to attract or please a man but as one of the
   essential aspects and pleasures of being human and being
   a woman

But after more conversations and after looking more
deeply at what was going on, I discovered that these three
qualities are just the most obvious manifestations of the real
secret shared by all these women.

What is this great secret? It is probably not what you
expect. It is certainly not transforming yourself into the
vapid, sexy bimbo it seems some guys are looking for. Doing
that, however, may be easy compared to what is really
required.

*The secret to finding a great relationship at age forty—or at
any age—is to be the woman you have always wanted to be.*

In most cases, this means being a person who is happy,
secure, generous, loving, accomplished, sensuous, and beautiful. Some of us may have achieved these ideals and will
have little trouble finding a wonderful love. Some of us
were once well on the way to being this kind of person, but
our development was interrupted by a demanding career,
the challenges of parenthood, or an unsuccessful marriage.
Or perhaps we were badly hurt by failures in past relationships or other areas of our lives, and our goals for ourselves
were set aside while we took care of the business at hand.

One thing I know for sure, none of us aspired to be bitter, cynical, distrustful, emotionally cold and hardened, and physically worn down or spent. Yet many women I meet who are after forty and single do seem cold and bitter. Granted, most of them are justified in being that way, and they can't wait to lay out the trials and tribulations that led them to where they are today. It is just that this attitude doesn't do them any good. Not only are men not interested in them or their tales of woe, but these women are not being who they once were on their way to being—the warm, loving person they know they still want to be and could be.

Fortunately, it is usually natural to get yourself back on track, because by doing so, you are merely being true to yourself. And all those detours and mistakes can turn out to be an advantage. After all, very few women in their twenties have had the experiences you have had. You see, the secret is not something you must do to hunt, trap, or catch a man. The secret is to get back to being yourself. If you can do that, finding a relationship will be a bonus, because you will already have won.

The Three Key Qualities to Develop

Now that you know the secret, let's talk about the three key qualities you need to focus on and develop to find and keep a truly great relationship.

At a dinner with five men who fit my own requirements for a great catch, I told them about these three qualities. Their responses were, "Bingo!" "Nita, you've struck gold."

"You have to let women know this." "I would love to date women closer to my age, but they're no fun. I'm sick of feeling that a woman is having sex just to accommodate my needs. I want her to want it, too." I've since shared these three qualities with more than a hundred men, and without exception, they have all agreed that these qualities are what they are looking for in a woman.

The response from single women after forty has been equally interesting. Most of the women I have talked to are embarrassed when I tell them about these qualities. Why? Because they realize that they need to wake up and start enjoying life again if they expect any man to enjoy them. As my friend Claire said, "After hearing this, I can see why I haven't been going out. I've been blaming the guys for being superficial, narcissistic, and intimidated by women, but the truth is, I wouldn't want to be with me either."

Not only is spending your time and energy on developing yourself in these three areas likely to pay big dividends when you are looking for a long-term relationship, but it will pay big dividends in your daily life as well, even if you never meet the man of your dreams. This is a game you can't lose.

Quality 1: Knowing—and Liking—Yourself

The most important quality in finding a nurturing and fulfilling relationship at any age is how you feel about yourself. When you feel happy, self-assured, and confident about who you are, that feeling is contagious. If you are Ms. Rejection-waiting-to-happen, it cannot help but affect how others look at you. And if you don't like yourself, you probably won't think much of a man who thinks you are great or be able to sustain a fulfilling relationship with him.

In addition to being someone you love, part of healthy self-esteem is having a life you love and are passionate about rather than waiting for a relationship before you wake up and start living your life.

A repeated complaint I hear from men is that they hate having a woman put her life into the man's hands. They want a woman who is already excited by her own life and wants to share that excitement and passion, not a woman who is looking for a man who will create a life for her. (Yes, there are men who want someone they can tell how to live and what to do or someone to mold to their vision. But these aren't men you would be interested in anyway.)

Divorced women often echo this complaint when they talk about having lost their sense of themselves in their marriage. To have any relationship work and last, you need to be strong enough to let the love of another person change you, inspire you, and contribute to your growth and expansion *without* losing your own sense of who you are. You truly need to have a sense of security and all-rightness about yourself to be able to let someone else into your life. I call it being your own person, and it is at the heart of healthy self-esteem.

My husband, Tony, and I went to Marrakech, Morocco, to celebrate my fortieth birthday. We stayed at La Mamounia, a former art deco palace that is now a luxury hotel.

Many of the guests are Parisians who come down for the weekend and spend most of their time sunbathing around the pool—topless. Although Tony and I spent most of our time sightseeing and exploring the wonders of the bazaar, we often ended up at the pool in the late afternoon. And I have to admit I was more entranced by the bathing beauties than Tony was. These Frenchwomen were not young, nor were they trying to look like young babes, but they were magnificent and had amazing bodies, every single one of them!

On the day of my birthday, staring at the parade of women, I became very depressed. Here I was, forty years old. I had been dieting and exercising for most of the last fifteen years, and I did not look (nor had I ever looked) like any of these women, and I realized I never would. In comparing myself to every woman who showed up at the pool, I began to feel ugly and worthless. And as I kept putting myself down, my fortieth birthday was rapidly becoming the worst day of my life.

Then I began to look at my life beyond just the shape of my body. It only took a moment for me to be filled with gratitude for the life I have. Just thinking of my family was enough for me to consider myself more blessed than I had ever hoped to be. Then I thought of the richness of my friendships, the adventures I have lived, the places I have traveled, the contributions I have made to others, my many amazing (at least to me) accomplishments, the fun I have had, and the love I experience every day. Overflowing with wondrous experiences, I realized I had lived a great forty years. I couldn't believe how lucky, fulfilled, and happy my life had been.

I realized that, on the positive side of the scale called "my life," I had enormous blessings, but I was willing to invalidate all that richness because I weighed fifteen pounds more than I wanted to! Just as the absurdity of that hit me, I also saw that I had not been living my life for myself at all. I was living a life in which I had to prove something and impress others. Both my parents were dead, but I was living in a house they would have approved of—one that would let them know I had done well. I had also given that power to certain friends and peers, who without knowing it or even saying a thing, influenced where I lived, what schools my kids went to, what clothes I thought were sophisticated, and so on. I couldn't think of anything in my life that was not filtered through what someone else would think.

At this point, I almost shouted out loud, "Whose life is this, anyhow?" That was the day I started living my own life. It was also the day I really became all right with who I am. It was the day I started to truly like myself.

Sometime later, I saw singer and actress Bette Midler being interviewed on television. She was being questioned about what it was like to be in a business that is dominated by incredibly good-looking women. The interviewer asked her to rate herself on a scale of one to ten against all the beautiful women in her business. I don't remember the exact number she gave in response, but it was way off the top end of the scale. I have often thought that this is the response each of us should strive to be able to give, not because we have inflated egos or ideas about who we are but because we know and appreciate our own value to ourselves and those in our lives.

Quality 2: Being Fun and Having Fun

It seems to me that the quality of being fun is practically extinct in both men and women after thirty. I know a lot of people who are satisfied and fulfilled. I know many who enjoy much of their lives—getting great pleasure from music, fine wines, reading a great book. When I ask people what they do for fun, the answers I get are usually something they feel good about doing, such as working out, writing in their journal, or cooking.

Now, I definitely like to do things that are satisfying and good for me, especially when I am checking them off my to-do list, but for me, that experience is quite distinct from playing and having fun.

Adults are often too adult to have fun, because we associate play and fun with being childish. But what is wrong with that? One of the women I interviewed who is over fifty and found a great relationship exemplifies this playfulness. Susan is refined and dignified. She has money, has traveled the world, has stayed in the finest places, and is used to comfort and good surroundings. As someone who really has "been there and done that," she could be—but isn't—a jaded snob.

Susan also never has trouble finding great men who want to be with her. And I know why. They want to be with her for the same reason I love to be with her: Susan is a kick. She has season tickets to the opera, which she is passionate about. But she is just as game to jump in the car to go camping and fishing. She is a great sport to be with and up for almost anything. The best thing about Susan is how excited she gets and how infectious her enthusiasm and joy are. Nothing is ordinary when you are with Susan, because she is as excited by life as a little kid. Susan has a ball, and anyone with her is going to have a ball, too.

Don't worry. If you haven't had fun in years, it is still not far away. There are two places to look: at the things you do that are just naturally fun for you and at everything else you are doing—particularly the things you have to do.

Horseback riding is something I do that is always fun for me. My friends joke about "that silly grin Nita gets the minute you put her on a horse." I don't "show" or compete, and I don't train in a certain style, though I love taking lessons when I can. I have no goals or ambitions. I ride because it is fun and I love it. I have been riding for years, and it works every time. Even if everything else in my life is grim, I can't help but be happy the second I get on a horse. This also happens to me when I ski and make love, where nothing else is going on but the sensations of the present.

So look for something that is to you what horseback riding is to me, something that takes you outside your head and the details of your life. Remember, this is not something that is "good for you" or for your development. This is something that is pure, unadulterated fun.

The next place to look for fun is in everything you are

already doing, especially in the things you have to do. It is easy to get caught up in the business of living—working, paying bills, doing chores, and managing the mundane details of life. At times, life can seem so burdensome that even planning a vacation becomes another item on the to-do list. Having "fun" isn't even on the agenda. Most of this is just simple forgetfulness. We not only forget that we can have fun, but we also forget that we possess the ability to *make* things fun. It only requires a slight change of attitude.

I run or do some kind of exercise every day. Running and bicycling are not fun for me, although they may be for someone else. Yes, I love the feeling I get afterward—the serenity and self-satisfaction last for the whole day—although in thirty years, I have never awakened excited about going for a run. Yet I have run in four marathons, and I not only felt a great sense of accomplishment at the end of each one, but I also found a way to have fun doing what, shortly after the first couple of miles, starts to seem like a really stupid idea and no fun at all. I line up a different friend to meet me at each six-mile interval and run with me. The job is not just to keep me company; each person has the assignment of saving up all his or her gossip for a few weeks beforehand in order to share it with me while we are running together. I cannot tell you how much fun the marathons have become. The most recent marathon, my friend Melissa had the last six miles with me. As she joined me, her words were not, "How are you doing?" or "Are you OK?" but "You won't believe what Laura said to Cheryl at the party last week." That was the only time I almost collapsed while running, because I was laughing so hard.

In my interviews with successful couples, without exception, they all say they had fun together from the very beginning. But you cannot wait to have a relationship before you have fun. People want to be with someone who is happy, someone who wants to play, someone who is, in fact, already playing. Remember Tom Sawyer painting the picket fence? It may seem "cool" to be blasé about life or too sophisticated to appreciate simple and silly things, but it is also very unattractive.

The statement that seemed most poignant when I interviewed a man about what he didn't like about older women was, "I am sick of being punished for what other men have done." Nothing puts more of a damper on fun (and is more unattractive) than cynicism and bitterness. We will discuss those two demons in Chapter 8, "Get Over It!"

Quality 3: Enjoying Sex

I devote a whole chapter later in the book to the role sex plays in finding and developing a lasting relationship. My point here is how attractive it is to men when a woman is comfortable with and enjoys her sexuality. I am not talking about being promiscuous, seductive, or even overtly sexy.

A woman who enjoys sex, who desires and gets pleasure from it, is a woman in possession of a quality men want—and want badly. Many women interpret this to mean that men just want sex badly, which is true to a point. But more to the point is that men, particularly men over the age of thirty-five or forty, are not just looking to get laid.

In interviewing and working with thousands of men, I have found no exception to one quality that never fails to turn them on—being with a woman who is turned on and deriving great pleasure out of being with that man. (Another one of men's great turn-ons is *giving* pleasure to a woman.)

In my experience, I have to say sex is an area in which almost never is the man at fault. He may need some feedback or coaching on how to please you, but his intentions are probably much purer than yours. If you have had a relationship in which you put up with sex, used it to get what you wanted, or merely accommodated your partner, you may be in need of some rehabilitation in this area.

Diane told me that nowhere in her sexual history did her physical sensations play a part. "It would be easy to blame this on the men and say that I just kept getting involved with jerks. But that wouldn't be the truth—this was my own doing. When I first started to have sex as a young girl, the gratification I got from it involved the feeling of being wanted or feeling attractive. This was very, very important to me. How stupid of me, but I really thought that, if a boy wanted to have sex with me, it meant I was desirable, lovable, beautiful. Now it's so ridiculously obvious that boys at that stage of life wanted to have sex with *anyone*—but probably, like many other girls, I grabbed at a guy's desire for sex to feed my own needs and insecurities. I doubt if I was physically or emotionally mature enough then to have derived any other pleasure from sex even if I had been looking for it. This also led to promiscuity on my part, because when you're looking outside of yourself for self-esteem, no matter how much you get, it isn't enough. So as I got older, I was very experienced, but in many ways I was still a virgin. I didn't even have an orgasm until I had been having sex for more than fifteen years!"

In Sharon's marriage, sex was something she did to ease the tension that built up after two or three weeks. "I can't blame my husband, because goodness knows he wanted to please me, but I just didn't want to let him. Because of other areas in our relationship, I didn't want to give him the satisfaction, or I didn't want to 'surrender' to the pleasure. After twenty years of this, I can't remember the pleasure available from sex, and to tell you the truth, I'm not interested."

What Sharon describes is true for many women in their late forties and fifties. When I tell women that enjoying sex is one of the secrets of finding a relationship, I often hear, "I have to enjoy sex? I don't think I could do it." "I have no interest in sex, but maybe I could develop that area." "I lost my interest in sex years ago." "Sex isn't very important to me anymore." Yet all the books I read about sex say women are in their prime at this age!

Sex is another area in which some work on your past may be necessary. You will shortcut this work when you stop blaming men and start looking at your part in the matter (and saying that your part is that you pick the wrong men is still blaming men). Most of the time, I find that women have been so busy using sex as a manipulation to get something else, they have missed out on what it really has to offer them. The good news is, it is not too late, but you must wake up to any of your tendencies and habits to use sex as a way to get something or to manipulate and how you may have disregarded the beauty and enjoyment of it.

What I love about these three qualities is that instead of an arsenal of seductive games or tricks, you just need to be yourself and enjoy life and sex. These are qualities you are certainly capable of developing and perfecting. More important, to the extent that you do embrace and embody these qualities, your life will be richer and more satisfying—with or without a partner!

tell the truth

In the minds of most of us, the word *single* does not apply to the average person over forty years old. Instead, it evokes an image of gen Xers, twenty-somethings, perhaps some cuties in their early thirties. The image of a forty-year-old woman or someone over fifty just doesn't fit.

I discovered this with my book *How Not to Stay Single* and at my seminars of the same name. I wrote that book for single people after thirty, thinking this would include those who are forty, fifty, or sixty. My seminars, however, are mostly made up of young people in their twenties and thirties, with a smattering of people after forty and very few people after fifty. I found out the reason for this: although many people in the higher age range want a relationship, they think the book or seminar is not meant for them. They hear the word *single*—which clearly and accurately describes their status—and it washes over them. They don't identify with "single"; they think I'm talking about someone else.

In fifteen years of giving seminars, I've found that the most common occurrence is a woman after forty waiting to talk to me at the end of the seminar about her highly unusual case. This "unusual" situation is as follows: "I've been married for twenty-two years and just got divorced. I met my spouse in high school, so I haven't really been on a date since then. I have no idea what to do or how to do it. I don't even know if I want a relationship. I don't know if what you have to say will apply to me because my situation is so different."

This *was* an unusual situation—thirty years ago! Nowadays, however, it is as common as a twenty-one-year-old woman wanting a relationship. With almost 55 percent of marriages ending in divorce, half of the people who are forty or older and were ever married are now divorced. So you are not alone out there. The good news is, you can learn from others' experiences and not have to reinvent the wheel. The bad news is, you have to do the same things someone who is thirty and has never been married has to do: you have to get out there, meet people, and socialize. You have to date. And guess what? Although you won't believe it, this is just as difficult for a twenty-eight-year-old as it is for you. I can't promise I will make getting back into the dating pool easier for you, but in Chapter 6, I will clearly tell you how to do it—yes, even at your age!

So if you are after forty or fifty or sixty or seventy, and you are interested in having a magnificent, fulfilling, and passionate relationship, this book is for you—not for your daughter or niece, but for you!

Yes, I Want a Relationship

The first step in the process of finding a relationship is simple. It is admitting you *want* a relationship, and part of this step is knowing it is all right to want one.

Most singles, especially women, have to deal with some embarrassment about wanting a relationship. In the past, women who didn't have a relationship were thought of as less than complete. Today, there is something of a backlash, so saying you want a relationship can now sometimes be interpreted as being "needy, desperate, and codependent." "You want a relationship? You must not be whole in yourself, or love yourself enough, that you need someone else to love you." "Women should be working on their careers or other loftier endeavors than pursuing a relationship. They are belittling their intelligence by having such a shallow goal or ambition." When you say you *want* a relationship, it gets translated into *need* whether you like it or not.

In addition, if you are after forty, there can be some embarrassment about being out there "looking" at your age. Carol, a friend who is fifty-four years old, told her thirty-year-old son she wanted a relationship and had decided to start dating. "It was as if I had said I was taking up a new career as a topless dancer! I hadn't seen that look of disgust on my son's face for a long, long time. But I remembered it clearly; it was the same look he gave me when he was nine years old and realized that his father and I did the thing that made babies. He actually was angry with me for considering such nonsense at my age."

Just as certain behaviors are forbidden to those deemed too young, women after a certain age aren't supposed to experience passion, aren't supposed to have dates and boyfriends, aren't supposed to make out, flirt, or act suggestive. Women still feel the need to prove they have substantial and worthwhile lives on their own. Men, on the other hand, can say at any age that they want a relationship without damaging their image. It is considered an aside and taken no more seriously than mentioning that they are taking up golf.

So the first step you need to take is to come clean with yourself about wanting a relationship. Forget what everyone else has to say about it. The fact that you want to love someone, that you want to be loved, is not something to be embarrassed about. It does not take away from your accomplishments and the other attributes of your life. Wanting a relationship is something very intimate, very personal, and is not in competition with your career. In fact, I have found that having the kind of love and support a relationship provides has made me more effective in my career and my relationships with other people. No matter how demanding, satisfying, and fulfilling your career is, it will not replace a relationship in your heart and soul. To want fulfillment in this area, to want to share your life with someone, is your choice. If it is what you want, then nothing should stop you from having it.

So if you do want a relationship, quit being embarrassed and defensive about wanting something so natural and normal. And if you don't want a relationship, that is also fine with me. My only question is, why are you wasting your time reading this book?

Here are some of the answers I have gotten when I asked women if they wanted a relationship: "I don't know if I really want a relationship, I've gotten so used to being on my own." "My marriage ruined me for all relationships, but I thought I'd read this just in case." Or my favorite, "I'm reading this for my daughter [friend, sister, or hairstylist]." The truth is, you haven't really given up on yourself, and I am glad you haven't, because I know you can have what you want.

The reason it is important not to be embarrassed about wanting a relationship is that the embarrassment hinders your ability to find one. If you are looking for an apartment to rent, you probably take advantage of all the resources available to you. You might ask all your friends, search the classifieds in the newspaper and on the Internet. You might go to a rental agent or realtor or even place a "wanted" ad yourself. If you are embarrassed by your situation, however, it will most likely stop you from using these services and thereby limit your choices and your effectiveness in finding a place to live.

If you think that wanting a relationship does *not* say something embarrassing or negative about you, you are much more likely to take advantage of all the options for finding the greatest and best match for you. (By the way, each of the resources mentioned for finding an apartment has a corresponding equivalent in finding a relationship. I wouldn't be surprised if the singles industry is even larger and more varied than the real estate business.)

Women constantly plead their case with me that the reason they don't have a relationship is because their standards are too high. Even their friends tell them they are too picky. My response usually surprises them, but it doesn't get them off the hook. I tell them they should be picky, and they should have very high standards. My goodness, they haven't done all this work on themselves; gone through all the adventures, education, and experiences in their lives; and made great lives for themselves only to give it all up for some guy who bores them, messes up the house, and shows them no appreciation. On the contrary, I expect that, at this time in your life, your standards should be extremely high. I firmly believe that if being with someone isn't going to make your life exponentially better, then don't bother. It *is* preferable to be alone than to wish you were.

Know What You Want

What is it you are looking for in a relationship? When I ask this question, what I usually get first is whatever is *not* wanted (which usually is everything that went wrong in the woman's last relationship). Then, when I repeat the question, I am offered a shopping list of attributes that some man must fulfill. Usually, it is a list of shallow requirements: height, weight, what kind of job he does, religion, presence or absence of facial hair, and financial standards.

While I am not belittling what you want in a man, it still doesn't answer the question. What do you want from a relationship?

From my interviews with women about what makes relationships better after forty, they each answered, without exception, that they know what they want and are now getting it. None of them were talking about the guy's eye color. Instead, they said things such as knowing they wanted to be with a man who had his own life and interests, instead of depending on the woman to fulfill him. They didn't necessarily want a man whose interests they shared, but a man "who had a life." The women wanted to feel nurtured and supported by a man, a man who will encourage a career, hobbies, and most important, support relationships with friends and family. They wanted a man who wanted to be with them but was not jealous or possessive of their time. They wanted qualities such as honesty, the ability to be intimate and close, and the desire to share his life, thoughts, and dreams.

So if you are going to be picky, which I highly recommend, then you need to have the widest possible range of men to go out with and pick from. And in order to go out with a lot of men, you need to meet even more men, because you are not likely to end up going out with every man you meet. So you have to take advantage of all the resources available to you, and you can't and won't do this if you are ashamed of what you want.

This may not seem like encouraging news, but really good news is not far off. The main point to come to grips with is that if you want a relationship, you can have it. I am not talking about just finding some "escort," but true love and passion, a relationship worth going for, worth fighting for—something better than any relationship you have ever had.

This requires you to step up to the plate, because as long as you remain in the dugout pondering your options, discussing the weather and field conditions, analyzing the competition, and arguing the politics of the game, the only guaranteed outcome is that you're going to get older.

face the facts

Before you take action to find a relationship, you have to come to grips with what you are dealing with. It is different to be dating at our age. Although a lot of things are better, there are also a lot of disadvantages and facts of which you should be aware.

Fact 1: It Isn't Easy, and You Never Feel Like It

Women often tell me they want a relationship but they don't like the dating scene. It is just not who they are, and it is not something they are comfortable with. Well, what a unique perspective! The truth is, *no one* likes the dating game; no one feels great about it or thinks it is a ball. I haven't yet met anyone who said, "Oh, dating, it's a blast. There's nothing I like to do more than get dressed up, meet a stranger, and have him judge and reject me in thirty seconds. Or even better, spend the evening with someone who wants to whine about how his 'ex' really screwed him, so do I mind paying for dinner?"

The only people I have met who think dating might be fun are married and haven't been on a date in ten or twelve years. They think you are having tons of romance and hot "action," when the truth is, they have simply forgotten what it was like.

Wanting a relationship without having to date is akin to wanting to get paid without having to work. It is fine to want this, but not very practical. And while we are at it, let's talk about comfort. So many women are not willing to go outside their "comfort zone," which is to say, they cannot do something they do not feel comfortable doing. As far as I can tell, comfort is being at home in a robe with no waist-band, watching a video or reading a book and eating. That is comfort, and nearly everything else is uncomfortable. So if you need dating to be comfortable before you give it a try, it is never going to happen.

It is interesting that we don't indulge ourselves in this "comfort" phenomenon in other areas of our lives. We would never tell a prospective employer we really want the job but are uncomfortable with the commute. But we have this myth about relationships that someday our prince will come and sweep us off our feet, and we won't have to do anything to make it happen.

For me, finding a relationship was not fun. Not once did I ever feel like going out and meeting new men. Not once! But just as I make myself exercise every day, I made myself go out three times a week. It was a discipline. Was it worth it? Are you kidding me? Never do I think of the horrible dates I had or the pain of rejection. It must be like what I hear about childbirth: somehow you forget the pain with the wonderment and love of the child.

Fact 2: You Have to Take Action to Find a Relationship

One of the biggest obstacles to finding a relationship is the idea that you are not supposed to *do* anything. Conventional wisdom says that a relationship will happen when you least expect it, when you are not looking for it but concentrating on something else. This is a complete fallacy, a myth, a fairy tale. It may be the plot line of a good many romantic novels and movies, but in reality, it is just not true.

Many years back, a Harvard/Yale study became the subject of major magazine articles and television programs throughout the country. The research was so shocking that it made the covers of *Time* and *Newsweek* in the same week. The highlight of the study was that a woman after forty had a greater chance of being hijacked by a terrorist than getting married. This news sent a good percentage of women and their mothers into a deep depression and made a best-seller out of my first book. Despite the boost to book sales, I couldn't believe these findings, so I did some research of my own and read the complete study. There I found some important information that had been skipped over in the major media coverage. The study stated that *if a woman took no action* to find a relationship and just waited for it to happen, then it was true that her chances of getting married were next to nil.

Still, the idea that great relationships "just happen" persists, and this false belief is preventing you from finding a relationship. Successful salespeople don't talk about their prospects' showing up "when the timing is right." You don't hear bankers or stockbrokers saying that they find the best investment opportunities when they are "not looking." Executives don't let the success of their companies "just happen." Yet many of these same people believe that a relationship will come along when they are not focusing on it. That is why so many people who are successful in their careers are unsuccessful in their love lives.

We understand that making something happen in our careers requires planning, perseverance, time, and hard work, but we think that finding a relationship shouldn't. We are enamored with the idea of fate's intervening and putting us in just the right place at just the right time to meet our true love. We think that if it is "meant to be," we will meet someone while we are walking the dog or by answering a wrong number.

Doing nothing to meet someone works better when you are young. Without our realizing it, a tremendous amount of socializing happened during our school years. Then, most of the people we met were in the same age group and single. To meet them, all you had to do was show up. Even studying was an opportunity to socialize. (Why do you think you studied in the library? Because it was quiet?) You met new people from morning until night, and, lo and behold, when you least expected it, when you were focused on something else, a relationship magically materialized.

Now you go to work and come home and wonder why relationships are not spontaneously happening as they are supposed to. You are waiting for the day you will get a message on your voice mail that says, "Hello. I'm the one. Please page me at the following number." Or maybe the UPS man is the prince you have been waiting for! If you look at the way you are living your life, this is how it is going to have to happen.

Another factor that made relationships seem to happen more easily then is that you probably attached less significance to them than you do now. You were more open. You didn't say, "I can't date someone in my English lit class! It might not work out, and then we'd still have to go to class together for the whole semester." Going out for a Coke was going out for a Coke, not your only hope of avoiding being alone for the rest of your life. No wonder relationships "just happened."

Of course, almost all of us are romantics. We have been taught by our culture that love should be magical, not something we engineer. And we all know one or two people for whom it happened just that way, which only serves to keep the myth going strong. But while you are waiting for fate to send you someone, you spend a lot of nights in the most unromantic way possible—alone. You may not like it, but the fact is that, statistically, staying at home and doing nothing is not a very good way to meet people.

Is how you meet someone really so important? Isn't it

more important that your relationship be romantic and magical after you get together? We forget that most of the romance in meeting someone is in the *story*, not in the circumstances. Once you have fallen in love, the fact that you met through a personal ad will also sound romantic and become another piece of the myth.

So you have to get out there and do something—not just when you feel like it, not when you have time, not when you lose weight and your hair grows out, but *now*.

Fact 3: Dating and Finding a Relationship Are Different after Forty

After people reach the age of forty, a relationship is not likely to involve the same kind of bonding instinct toward starting a family and building your adult lives together. By forty, most people have already established themselves in their careers. They have probably already had their children and are often somewhat limited by these two facets of their lives. For example, they may not be able to relocate easily or even have the same time schedules as the person they are dating. The "blending" of lives can be much more complicated at forty-eight than at twenty-five.

Besides all the other difficulties of forming a foundation of a relationship and overcoming the obstacles of intimacy, you usually have a lot more logistics to handle, too. A friend of mine recently fell in love with a man who lives across the country from her. They are fortunate, since both their careers involve a great deal of travel on both coasts. Even though it would be possible for them to live in the same city, they enjoy sharing each other's homes, families, and the communities they love and feel connected to. My friend had been away from her apartment for several weeks living with her boyfriend. They went back to her place, and she was walking around her home kind of fussing with her stuff and reclaiming her space. Her boyfriend noticed and remarked, "You really love being in your own home, don't you?" So even when the logistics can be handled fairly easily, it is still complicated to include another person.

It is different developing a relationship at our age, and it should be. Surely something has happened, evolved, developed while you were living your life the past twenty years! Everyone is always talking about the baggage people bring to relationships. I don't know why baggage has such a negative connotation. To me, baggage means that this person has lived, has loved, has had experiences, problems, situations, relationships. I happen to think this is a good thing. A man who has had a life before meeting me is much more interesting than one who has been waiting for me to give him a life.

I just love it when a woman tells me about her new relationship and how things are on hold because the man has a lot of baggage to "let go of" or "get rid of." I am always curious about the method by which this can be accomplished: hypnosis? lobotomy? I advise women who want a man without baggage to date a twelve-year-old; otherwise, it is pretty hopeless. And by the way, how many of you are coming without your own matched set of luggage?

Not only is it different to be dating and relating at our age; it can and should be better, too. Like a fine wine, so many more textures, fragrances, and subtleties only become available with the passage of time.

Fact 4: Regarding Age and Aging, Women Are at a Disadvantage

While a fifty-year-old man can very often date a thirty-five-year-old woman, the reverse is not as common. One woman after fifty who looks much younger reports being on a date with a fifty-six-year-old man. He was telling her about some of his recent blind dates. He started laughing and said, "You won't believe this, but I've had friends fix me up with fifty-year-old women! What were they thinking?" He was incredulous about even considering going out with a woman so old.

My husband, Tony, and I were at a party recently. As we were dancing, Tony looked around at the other couples on the dance floor and whispered to me, "It sure seems like there are a lot of old farts here with young babes." I looked around, and what I saw confirmed his observation. I told Tony that if something happened to me, I thought he, too, would go after a much younger woman. He wasn't so sure. "Why do you think I would date someone so young?" he asked. My reply: "Because you could."

It is generally true that what a man looks for first in a woman is good looks. And for the most part, women look better when they are younger. Of course, some people get better looking as they age, and there are some men who prefer a more mature look, but the vast majority of men like young, fresh, hard bodies. Not only is this visually more pleasing to many men, but it also gives them ego points— from which stem the phrases *trophy babe* and *arm candy*.

When I told Tony he could get a young babe, his face lit up. "Really? I could? Will you tell me how?" It was amusing (for about a second), but what was exciting Tony was the prestige he felt at the idea that *he* could be seen with one of "those." It was not the thought of what a wonderful relationship he could have with someone so young (at least, that is what he told me).

Sara, a fifty-two-year-old single, attractive artist who has no trouble finding dates, told me, "It's easy for me to date. I learned a few years ago to just never tell men my age." I was troubled by this response. I have always thought that lying about your age makes you seem embarrassed, and it makes you look old for the age you say you are. I also think lying and deceit have no place in a relationship. I told Sara all this, and she said she had always felt the same way. She really is quite beautiful and very comfortable with who she is, but she has found that as soon as a man hears her age, *even a man who is older than she*, he stops taking her seriously as a potential date!

Most of us do not like to hear this—I certainly don't— but it is a reality. There are a couple of ways to deal with this reality. One is to give up and enter a convent. "It's stupid to even think of dating. All the men I'm interested in only want a twenty-year-old, and the men who are interested in me are so old that my life would resemble that of a geriatric nurse. No, thank you. I'm fine on my own."

This "whine" is unoriginal, as well as unproductive and self-destructive. It may be a fact that women of a certain age are at a disadvantage in finding a relationship, but I have seen many women after forty years of age who knew the secret to overcoming this so-called obstacle. For instance, the woman I mentioned earlier who had a date with the man who wouldn't consider going out with a fifty-year-old woman is now in a fabulous relationship with a man in his fifties. Dave is good-looking and successful, but more important, he is a great and decent man who told me he would no more think of going out with a thirty-year-old than he would a ten-year-old. And he knows he has the choice.

What I learned from Dave and the other "success" stories of women after forty is:

> *The men who are looking for a relationship with a thirty-year-old, who want and need the ego points, don't want a relationship with you, and the men who have to have that kind of relationship, you don't want.*

Instead of something to whine about, this is great news.

The bad news is that the whining gives you another excuse not to do something about finding a relationship. And it gives you a cover-up for what is the greatest and most difficult-to-face obstacle—*rejection*.

Fact 5: To Find a Relationship, You Are Going to Have to Endure a Lot of Rejection

You don't want to hear this. You hate rejection and want to find a way to avoid it. My response is, "You've mastered that." What I have learned is that people have organized their lives so they can avoid being rejected—usually, by not putting themselves out there in the first place.

When I talk to most singles about the need to get out and meet people in order to find a relationship, the most common answer is, "I don't have time." I don't think anyone is lying to me about how busy they are. Except these are the same women who are out at 5:00 A.M. running and lifting weights before they wake up the kids, do two loads of laundry, pack lunches, and go to work. We all know that if you want something done, give the task to a busy person. So I don't buy that they are too busy to socialize.

The bad news is, if you want to find a relationship, there is no way around rejection. You will have to go through it again and again and again and again. It comes with the territory. The good news is, you can learn to deal with rejection more effectively and get through it with a lot less pain than you think.

Less than 3 percent of the people in my seminars say their personality comes across on a first date. Odds are, you are among the more than 97 percent who don't. So basically, you are being rejected, and the other person doesn't even know who you are. So chances are, the rejection you experience is not personal; you are being rejected for arbitrary reasons. We all use superficial and personal criteria to evaluate others. When you realize that the reason he didn't smile at you was because of your hair color or that he lost interest in the conversation because he found out you smoke, how can you take it personally?

Once you understand how arbitrary most rejection is, you won't spend so much time recovering from it. Most time spent focusing on emotional wounds or analyzing what happened is wasted time. You need to get over rejection as quickly as possible. Remember, you are going to have to go through a lot of people to find one who is right for you. You have high standards, and so do other people. And a lot of people simply won't like you. It is not important to know why someone didn't like you. You just need to get over it and get on to the next person.

It is important, however, to know *when* you are being rejected, and that is not always obvious. Almost never will a man say, "I don't want to go out with you because I really don't like you." He will make up an excuse: "It's tax season," or "I have relatives coming in from out of town." My rule of thumb: If he is not making time for you, consider yourself rejected. This is a time when actions speak louder than words. Clinging to the remote possibility that someone might be available in a few months won't get you any closer to this person who doesn't really like you, and it will postpone your being with someone who does.

I am telling you, if he is interested, he will make time. If Cindy Crawford or Demi Moore were in town and wanted to go out, believe me, he would file for an extension on his taxes and make the relatives fend for themselves for one night.

You really have to get this, because living on hope is very unproductive. I have heard so many stories from women telling me there was a man in her life, but he has a big project at work, and when it is over, they will be seeing each other. Are you kidding me? Do you want to know how many of these situations actually ended in a real relationship? None. Even if your situation is for real, in the meantime get out and meet other men, now!!

The point is, if they are not interested, they won't tell you directly. They will handle it by doing what you do when you don't want to be with someone—by not making time.

Once you know how to tell when you have been rejected, you need to know how to deal with the pain. Rejection hurts, and pretending it doesn't isn't going to help you achieve your goal. There is, however, a fine line between feeling the disappointment of rejection and wallowing in the pain you feel. People often use the fact that they were rejected to avoid opening up again. They take time off from relationships to analyze what went wrong. They have to go through every date, every phone call, to figure out when it happened, what happened, what mistakes took place. Most of their analysis is unproductive.

You want to know what went wrong, what happened? He didn't like you. In my book *How Not to Screw It Up*, I say that one of the key ingredients to a wonderful relationship is to be with someone who likes you. So get over it. Don't look for hidden meanings. In relationships as in horseback riding, when you fall, the thing to do is get right back on the horse.

Another mistake people often make is to justify rejection in an attempt to avoid the pain. I have heard too many women say, "I'm powerful, and it intimidates men." I don't find this information useful. It certainly won't keep you warm at night.

The biggest mistake to make regarding rejection is to try to change yourself in order not to be rejected. I personally had more first dates with no second dates than anyone I have ever met. I must have experienced every possible nuance of rejection there is. It was obvious to me I was doing something wrong. My solution was to change. I would replace the old Nita with a new, improved, nonrejectable model.

First, I asked my girlfriends for their analysis and advice. They told me the old "You are powerful, and men are intimidated by you" mantra. Which wasn't too helpful. So I managed to find a few of the men who had rejected me (interesting how hard it is to find a man who has rejected you; they seem to disappear) and quizzed them on the subject. They said I was "loud and pushy." Fascinating, and a little different interpretation from "powerful and intimidating."

It seemed pretty obvious that men don't like "loud and pushy," so I decided to become demure. Now, I had as much chance of becoming demure as Shaquille O'Neal has of becoming petite. Even if I could have pulled it off, becoming something or someone else wasn't the solution to my problem. What I really needed was to find someone who liked "loud and pushy." Granted, there aren't very many men who do, but fortunately, all I needed was one.

A woman who took my seminar in Phoenix had a unique problem. "I make a lot of money," she said. "My income is in the top 5 percent of the country. I'm very successful, but I find that men can't handle it. Even men who make a lot of money themselves don't like it when a woman is too successful. What should I do?" I told her to give me all her money. But seriously, I agreed with her. A lot of men can't handle being with extremely successful women. But, I reminded her, she was only looking for one who could. That night a lot of men came up to her and said they would like to interview for the part. Why would you give up something great about yourself to find a relationship? Who would want that relationship?

At one point during the period before I met my husband, Tony, I was so sick of rejection that I just gave up. I said the same things you have probably said: "What am I doing? This is awful. Besides, I have great friends. I don't need a relationship. I'm fine on my own. I'm not going out anymore." These were good arguments. My roommate was convinced. I even believed them—for a while. But after a couple of days, it dawned on me. I thought, "If I quit now, I will probably live the rest of my life alone."

So I climbed back on the horse. Within a couple of weeks, I met a man I really liked. We went out for several weeks, and I thought, "This might be it." Then we spent an incredible weekend skiing together, and I was sure he was "the one." The weekend must have been a turning point for him, too. On Sunday, our idyllic trip was cut short when he told me that he had decided to go back to his ex-girlfriend. A single thought rang in my head: *"Quit!"*

That night, I was despondent. I knew I needed to go out and meet someone new, but I had really hit rock bottom. I was so depressed that I didn't just want to crawl into my bed, I wanted to crawl under it.

Somehow I managed to get myself dressed, made up, and out of the house. I reminded myself I needed to go someplace where I could meet people, not some quiet restaurant where I could sit in a dark corner and drown my sorrow in a Diet Pepsi. I halfheartedly chose a local bar. That was the night I met Tony.

Once I met Tony, I could look back on my relationships with other men from a different perspective. I had to go through a lot of people to find him—a lot. But in retrospect, I could see that every one of the men who had rejected me had done me a service, because with each rejection from Mr. Wrong, I got one step closer to Mr. Right. If I had quit when it hurt too much, I would have quit one step short of my goal. The temptation to shut down was great, but if I had let frustration win, I would have missed out on the love of my life.

By the way, there is one other *very* effective way of handling rejection, but it is not for the fainthearted. If you really like someone and you think this person has rejected you for the wrong reasons, or wouldn't reject you if he or she got to know you better, reject the rejection!

When people reject you, they expect you to become pitiful and pathetic, to fall apart before their eyes. A confident reaction is the last thing they expect. When you respond by telling them that they have made a mistake and you know they would really like you if they spent more time with you, it really throws them. Self-esteem is very attractive. They will think twice—and they will probably give you a second chance.

This is exactly what Tony did after I decided he was not my type and turned down his request for a second date. Instead of accepting my rejection, he called me back and asked me out again. When I asked him later why he did that, he said he wanted to give me another chance. Tony may be quiet and shy, but he has very high self-esteem. And when he gave me that response, I was impressed.

I can hear you saying, "No way. I could never do that." But if you are like the more than 90 percent of the people in my seminars and don't make a quick, good first impression, you are going to have to do this. If you really like someone and think that once that person got to know you, she or he would feel differently, why not risk it? What have you got to lose? After all, this is a person who has already rejected you.

Relationships aren't designed for "playing it safe." When it is safe is when you don't care. The minute you care, it is no longer safe, because you can be hurt. But only at that point is it possible for you to have a meaningful relationship. You can't wait until you are sure it is going to work out before you open up. You can't say, "I won't get close until I know he is right for me," because the only way you are going to discover whether he is right for you is by getting close.

go for the real thing

A familiar refrain of women after forty is, "I'd rather be alone than settle for less than what I want. I'm too picky. I have high standards, and that's why I don't have a relationship."

I am in full agreement with the first part of this declaration. You shouldn't settle; you should have very, very high standards, and it is important to be picky. That, however, is not the reason you don't have a relationship.

When we think of settling, we usually think of hanging on to a relationship that clearly isn't "it" but seems better than nothing. Of course, it is nice to have a companion, an escort, not to be a "lonely" woman at the party. It is wonderful to have friends, and certainly to have male friends, to do things with. That is not what I am talking about here. I mean the kind of relationship in which you are keeping someone around until the "real" one comes along. It may seem to make perfect sense, but this "filler" relationship actually prevents you from having the one you want.

My close friend Gale was dating Larry, a great guy she had met soon after her divorce. After she had dated him for several months, I asked her over lunch if this was it. We had a conversation that unfortunately was repeated many times over the next seven years. "He's a wonderful man, but I don't feel like I want to marry him. He's smart, successful, kind, great with the kids, sex is good, and I have a wonderful time with him. There's nothing wrong with him, but I don't feel the something else that I think should be there to want to marry him."

By the third time we had this conversation, I told her that if she didn't feel it by now, she wasn't going to and she should move on. She deserved more, and the truth is that, although Larry was wild about her, he deserved more. Meaning he deserved someone who was wild about him. But Gale could not let go because "there's nothing wrong with him, and maybe this is what love is like at our age. Maybe you don't feel that passion, that knowing that you want to be with that person and spend the rest of your life with him?" How depressing!

I argued with her for years. I told her that Larry was a great guy and she didn't have to find something wrong with him in order to justify not marrying him. Meanwhile, she kept putting off the subject of marriage with him. She asked, "How do you know if you want to marry someone? Maybe my first marriage has ruined me for ever wanting to get married again." I told her what I have told so many others: if, after six months to a year, you don't know that you love and want to be with a man, then you don't. (She was by then five years into the relationship.) But she couldn't let go of the comfort, the convenience, the company. Finally, after seven years, Larry gave up. He broke it off; he knew he wanted more, and it wasn't happening with Gale.

At first, she was devastated! I had never seen her look so distraught. But soon she started dating again, and within six months, a friend fixed her up with Paul. It didn't take her a week before she had feelings about Paul that she had never had with Larry. She knew, he knew, and four months later, they were married. It was a joyous event. They are one of the best-suited, most happily married couples I know, married for six years now.

I didn't have to tell Gale I told you so, because she came to me to express her regret. Of course, she was upset that she had "settled" for so long and cheated herself out of the real thing, but mostly she was sorry to have taken that time from Larry. Fortunately, he, too, ended up in a great marriage.

"I know we can't undo the past, and Larry is not a victim, but, Nita, put this in your next book so others can learn from my mistakes."

When I tell people it is important to be available in order to find a relationship, they usually couldn't agree more. They are angry that so many people who are unavailable are out there dating, pretending to be available. They are afraid of becoming the unsuspecting victim of such a detestable person. They want advice on how to recognize and identify people who are unavailable so they can steer clear of them.

Then I ask them whether they are available. Sometimes they get a little defensive: "Of course, I'm available. I'm looking for a relationship. I'm open to finding the right person. I'm taking this seminar, aren't I?"

Let's find out what you think. The following stories are from people who have taken my seminars. Which of these four people do you consider to be available?

Story 1: *"I'm waiting for the right person to show up, but I'm not going to waste my time with someone who doesn't have what I'm looking for. He has to be financially independent, not smoke, be in good shape, have a great sense of humor, and not mind when I spend time with my friends. Find me someone like that and I'll jump at the chance to get involved with him."*

Story 2: *"I know he doesn't love me now. But we have a good time, and he shows signs that he cares. He wouldn't keep going out with me if he didn't really like me. In fact, I think he's just afraid to admit how much he cares. If I keep hanging in there and make it safe for him, I know he'll come around. In the meantime, if I meet a better man, I'll end it."*

Story 3: *"I was in denial, but now I realize he's never going to leave his wife. I love him, and I know he loves me, too, but there's no future in it. That's why I want to meet someone else. I'm open to dating, but until someone great comes along, at least there is someone who fulfills my needs."*

Story 4: *"I'm hoping Mr. Right will come along. In the meantime, being single can be lonely, and I'm seeing this other guy. He's nice and sweet and really likes me. I know he would like it to be more, and sometimes I worry about leading him on, but I've told him the truth: there's no future in this relationship. I think of him as a friend I can have sex with. When I get lonely or need an escort, he's there for me."*

These four women have one thing in common—with one another and with a majority of other single women: they think they are available, but, really, they aren't. They took my seminar in the hope that it would help them find mates. It was a rude awakening for them to realize that it was their own unavailability that prevented them from finding the kind of relationships they wanted.

These four stories typify the situations I hear about most often from people in my seminars. Let's analyze what makes these people unavailable.

Number 1 is looking for the perfect man, but she will never find him. It is not too hard to imagine that even if she miraculously met someone who lived up to her impossible criteria, he would still somehow fall short of her ideal of perfection. You should know that if you are unwilling to go out and meet new people or to spend time with anyone who isn't "perfect," you are not available.

The remaining three stories are about women who are

unavailable because they are already in relationships. Being in a dead-end, or "go-nowhere," relationship is by far the most prevalent circumstance preventing people from finding someone with whom they could have a real relationship, which is why we are going to explore this phenomenon in detail.

When you are in a dead-end relationship, you are not available. It is kind of like this: if the seat next to you on the bus is taken, no one is going to sit down in it. I can't tell you how many people I have known who insisted they were "open" despite being in a go-nowhere relationship. They didn't meet anyone new, however, until they broke up with their dead-end lovers.

There are several kinds of go-nowhere relationships. Many women, like those in stories 2 and 3, are involved with people who are unavailable. If you are involved with someone who is unavailable, stop hoping his situation will change and move on. By staying with this person, you are virtually guaranteeing that you will not find someone with whom you could have a truly satisfying relationship.

If you are going out with someone who is married, you are doubly sabotaging yourself, because being in this relationship contributes to your not feeling good about yourself. You do not hold some cherished and special place in your lover's life. It is more likely a second-best, runner-up, on-the-sidelines type of relationship, no position from which you will feel great about your role or yourself. Also, I am a big proponent of marriage. It is obviously not supportive of marriages if you are in any way undermining one.

People often justify going out with someone who is married by saying things like, "His marriage was already over," or "He's just staying with her because of the kids." It is not an expression of love to be with someone whose integrity is compromised because he is messing around outside his marriage. If the marriage is about to end, if he and his wife are going to get divorced, then tell him to handle it and then call you. You can even tell him you love him and want to be with him, but also tell him to clean it up with his wife before being with you. Even if you are not the cause of the marriage's breaking up, being with a married person corrodes your sense of self-worth. And self-esteem, as I say throughout this book, is a prerequisite for a good relationship.

Story 4 is from a woman who was involved in a close, sexual relationship with a guy to whom she had no intention of committing. This can be the most difficult kind of relationship to give up.

No one has ever fought me on this harder than Cynthia, a forty-seven-year-old management consultant who took my seminar several years ago. Convincing her to stop seeing Randy, a guy with whom she had been having a go-nowhere relationship for the previous three years, was like trying to pry a life preserver away from someone who was drowning.

Cynthia was quite a bit older than Randy, and she knew she would never want to marry him, but she hated the dating scene and didn't want to face the possibility of being rejected. Randy adored her and was always there for her. It wasn't easy, but I finally convinced her to break up with him.

As she was soon to find out, breaking up wasn't enough. Shortly after they stopped seeing each other, Randy ran into some problems in his application to graduate school. He called her for help. She wanted to be his friend, so she agreed to get together with him. You can probably guess what happened. It was late, it was so nice seeing each other again, blah, blah, blah. Anyway, they got back together.

Three months later, she broke it off again. Again, he had an emergency. Again, he called her. Again, she wanted to be a friend. Again, seeing each other brought them back together. The same cycle occurred one more time before I was finally able to convince Cynthia that she had to stop being Randy's "friend." She saw that to be truly supportive, she would have to get out of his life; that by being there to bail him out of emergencies, she was making it impossible for either of them to move on.

She had broken up with him before; this time she gave him up. The loss was very painful, but eventually, things worked out for everyone involved. Cynthia found a guy she was crazy about and married him. Randy, when he realized Cynthia really wasn't coming back, stopped hoping she would and stopped having emergencies. He found a woman who adores him. Now that they each have mates, Randy and Cynthia still stay in touch. They have a genuine friendship.

Your dead-end lover will probably want to "stay friends" when you tell him you want to break up. Be a true friend and explain why this has to be done cold turkey. Explain that you will be able to resume the friendship after you have both found other mates. Realize that merely saying the words is not going to get your point across. You are going to have to withdraw from the relationship, no matter how painful that may be for you or the other person. You are doing your "friend" a disservice by leading him on.

People give me all kinds of reasons why they shouldn't have to break up with their dead-end lovers:

"We're really just friends."

"He knows I go out with other men, and it's OK."

"I've been seeing him for five years, and I've had several other relationships in between."

"At my age, this is as good as it gets."

The real reason you cling to dead-end relationships is because you are afraid that nothing better will come along and you will be alone. You want to wait until you find a replacement before you let go because you are afraid there will be a void in your life. You should understand that a genuine relationship is most likely to occur when there is just such a void.

If you are afraid of being alone, that is all the more reason to give up your dead-end relationship. If you want to have a great relationship, it is important that you find out you can live successfully without one.

Yes, you will be taking a risk if you give up your dead-end lover. There is no guarantee you will find someone to replace him. But think about what you are giving up by staying with that person. Think about the relationship you envision, the one that would fully nurture and satisfy you. That is what you really want, and that is what you will probably never have if you don't take the risk. Your project of finding a lifetime mate is going to require you to take a lot of risks, so you may as well start getting in the habit now.

Once you are sure of your own availability, it is time to focus on the people you date. How can you ensure that you won't get involved with someone who is unavailable? With most people, it is pretty straightforward. Someone who is married is *not* available. A person who is living with someone or already in a long-term relationship is *not* available.

People who are separated or recently divorced are not quite as unavailable as those who are married. But they are often still focused on their ex and may be embroiled in legal and financial matters as well. It isn't a hard-and-fast rule, but you should know that the median remarriage time for someone who has been divorced is forty-four months. A better rule of thumb than elapsed time is the amount of time a person spends talking about his ex.

If you are dating someone who is still getting over a former lover, don't allow yourself to be drawn into the process by engaging in extended conversations, dispensing advice, or being a shoulder for him to cry on. Instead, simply say that you don't feel comfortable talking about this. Otherwise, you risk becoming associated with the old relationship, and when your lover finally does get over it, he will have to leave you, too, in order to move on.

What if someone's words about his availability contradict his actions? In this case, it is usually best to believe the actions. An excellent guideline to help you determine whether someone is available is how much time he is spending with you. Basically, someone who cannot or does not make time to be with you is not available despite his protestations to the contrary.

The opposite can also be true, as my friend Sharon discovered. She was dating a man who kept telling her he didn't want to get involved: he was married to his career; he wasn't interested in a relationship; he wasn't ready for a commitment; she shouldn't get her hopes up. Despite this running dialogue, he called her nearly every day, they saw each other almost every night, and he asked her to go on a vacation with him.

Sharon, believing what he said about his unavailability, almost broke up with him. I told her that I had never seen anyone who was more available and that she should pay attention to his actions, not his words. She hung in there, and eventually they got married.

When my friend Sue moved in with her boyfriend, he warned her that he definitely had no intention of ever getting married. Her response was, "I don't remember asking you." She never brought it up again, but he did when he proposed a year later.

A lot of people who really do want to get involved in permanent relationships think and say that they don't because they are afraid. That they have fears about getting more deeply involved doesn't necessarily mean they are unavailable. After all, many of the men and women who are now married and thrilled about it were once just as apprehensive.

If a man says he doesn't want a relationship but his actions tell you he does, don't give up on him too soon. Obviously, there will be a time when giving up on such a man becomes appropriate, but a lot of people make the mistake of doing this prematurely.

It is also possible to get comfortable enough in your life without a relationship to avoid experiencing the discomfort of whatever pain or loneliness may still be there. Most of us have organized our lives and thinking, at least subconsciously, around avoiding pain and rejection. We justify not going out and risking rejection by being resigned and cynical, saying there are no good men, they just want sex or a younger woman, or they don't meet our standards. All this is pretty convincing. The problem is, this mantra only lulls you into doing nothing. In the long run, comfort, convenience, and compromise are much too costly.

I have always traveled, and I love the fantasy of meeting someone because he happens to be seated next to you on the plane. In fact, one woman who took my course in Los Angeles said she wouldn't be able to do her homework (smiling at men) that week because she had to go on a business trip. I told her to smile at men on the plane. She is now married to the guy who was in seat 11B. If she had filled that seat with her good traveling buddy, however, she would probably not have met the love of her life. Not only would the seat have been taken; she wouldn't have been looking.

When I was in the process of finding a relationship, I learned to use the pain of loneliness to motivate me. One of my worst moments was being at a big New Year's Eve party. The clock struck midnight, and everyone except me was kissing someone. It only lasted a moment, because I soon got many second- and third-tier kisses, but it was awful! I swore I was never going to go through that again. There were two options: I would never celebrate New Year's again or—and this was the option I chose—I was going to have a love by the next New Year's Eve. I failed to achieve that goal, because it was two years before I met Tony, but the experience got me into action and kept me going until it eventually worked.

People always ask, "What if I put myself out there and I get hurt?" Then guess what? You will get hurt. It will only make the victory sweeter when it happens. It has been nineteen years since I met Tony, but I still remember what it was like to be living my life alone, and I still don't take it for granted that I now share my life with someone I love.

Get Yourself the Support You Need

Looking for a relationship is not easy. We have already covered why it is so embarrassing to admit to yourself that you want a relationship, let alone to let others know you are actually looking! "Oh, no! Another woman on the hunt! Beware of traps, seduction, and manipulation." No one wants to be seen in the unflattering light of being a predator.

Years ago, in my work as a management consultant, I discovered that it was usually only the most successful businesspeople who hired consultants. There was a direct relationship between a person's degree of success and his or her willingness to seek consultants and outside support. Today, the "I can do it on my own" attitude is virtually nonexistent among powerful business executives.

The same is true of sports. Of course, team sports are always coached, but also at every big individual event from tennis to horse jumping, you find that the athletes work with personal coaches or trainers. Many amateurs train on their own, but you will never see world-class athletes without a coach.

To succeed in finding a relationship, you need to make it a priority. Part of this is getting support for yourself. When I take on a project, I usually find one of two kinds of support available—the "hallelujah choir" or the "Greek chorus." Unfortunately, the Greek chorus tends to be the most readily available, often without your even having to ask for it. It sounds like this: "Oh, you're looking for a relationship? You don't need that; you have close friends who love you. You are too 'mature.' There are no good men out there. All the good men are __ [taken, looking for a younger woman, spoiled]. There are no good men in __ [Seattle, New York, Atlanta, Zanzibar]. Maybe you should get some therapy instead so that you love yourself."

The hallelujah chorus, though more difficult to locate and recruit, is obviously what you are looking for. Their song is much different: "Sure you can find someone. Get off your butt and do something. I don't want to hear your __ [whines, complaints, excuses]. Don't give up!"

I recommend that you not even mention your project to someone you are pretty certain will be part of the Greek chorus. When a baby is just learning to walk, the parents make a big deal about every move the baby makes that even looks like a step. I have never heard a mom or dad say, "Oh, gravity is tough. Maybe you should wait until you're older and won't fall. Perhaps you should be satisfied with crawling so you won't have to worry about those dangerous tumbles."

In this project, you are a baby. You only want to talk about finding a relationship with those people who will applaud and support you. You don't need to be defending yourself all the time. It is difficult enough without having to justify yourself to others every step of the way. This doesn't mean you should stop talking with or give up friends who won't understand and support what you are up to; just don't share this particular project with them in its infancy stage.

My children are adopted. Tony and I found out about our first child three weeks before he was born. One night, a week before he was due, my best friend, Terry, took me shopping to prepare for his arrival. We were both terribly excited about this baby. Terry kept asking me if I had told different people about the baby and what their responses had been, but I had shared our news with very few people. She finally asked why, if I was so excited, hadn't I shared it with these friends and family. I told her, "I don't want to deal with their stuff about adoption." She was a little puzzled but let it go.

We had a big mission to accomplish that night, so we went on with choosing baby shampoo and Snuglis. At the checkout counter at our last stop, the clerk at the cash register said sweetly, "Looks like someone is having a baby." Terry proudly pointed to me and said, "Any day now." Fortunately, I didn't look the least bit pregnant, so the clerk looked quite puzzled. When I told her I was adopting, she responded, "Oh, that's too bad. Aren't you worried about the mother changing her mind?" At that point, Terry said, "Now I get it."

Having a friend like Terry really made getting ready for being a mom much easier. In this project of finding a relationship, you also need support. Just be picky about whom you choose. Find at least one person whom you know will want you to have what you want and won't give up on you even when you do.

This advice to get yourself supported is in all my books and courses. Over the years, from the feedback I have gotten, I am more convinced than ever how important it is. Some of the best teams have been a daughter supporting her mother (or the reverse), associates from work (of either sex), and two people supporting each other in the same project. You don't even need to limit yourself to one person. Looking for a needle in a haystack (which, for some of you, may be what this seems like) goes a lot faster with ten people than with only one or two.

clean up your act

This chapter is about being attractive—about being the kind of person someone else would love to be with, about presenting yourself in a way that makes you someone a man is interested in meeting and getting to know better.

Attraction is that initial "hit" that makes us want to find out more about another person. Attraction is mostly related to appearance and how we look to another, which I talk about later in this chapter. But there are other, not-so-obvious features that strongly influence whether a man will be attracted to you or not.

The first step in being attractive is for you to get that you really have something special to offer. Nothing is more attractive than a woman who thinks highly of herself. This is not to be confused with being stuck-up or conceited. It is just that we tend to be most critical of ourselves—and goodness knows, nobody knows our faults better than we do. If, knowing all this, you still like yourself, you must be a good person, and other people will pick that up from you. A man would be smart and damn lucky to be with you. And it is surprising how much that inner confidence projects to others.

I always ask people in my seminars to make a list of the ten things they think make them a great catch. They complain and moan and say, "You've got to be kidding!" *They can't think of ten things*. But if I ask them to make a list of what they are looking for in a mate, they can fill ten pages in five minutes. In my opinion, this second list is useless, since most people really don't know what they want in a relationship (we will talk more about this in Chapter 7).

The useful list is the list in which you begin to see what *you* have to offer someone else. Why would someone think you are great? You need to be honest here, not modest, and look for the treasures within yourself. You may also develop new wonderful qualities, but for now, begin with what you have.

Work on Your Self-Esteem

Remember from Chapter 1 that self-esteem is one of the primary components of the secret. Men are attracted to women who know who they are and who like themselves. In fact, we all are. It is often said that until you love yourself, you can't love anyone else. I believe that unless you love yourself, you won't let anyone else love you. Having high self-esteem is essential not only to attracting people but to maintaining a great relationship once you do find someone. A lack of confidence in yourself can be contagious, as I discovered one night shortly after Tony and I began living together.

Tony had come home from a "night out with the guys." He told me about a woman who had flirted with him at the bar where he and his friends had spent the evening. He was not talking about this woman to make me jealous; he was just telling me about his night. It was clear that he had no interest in her. Nevertheless, hearing about this woman made me start to feel insecure about myself.

"Was she really pretty?" I asked him. "She was thinner than I am, wasn't she? I'll bet your friends thought you were a fool not to get her phone number."

As I expressed these insecurities, I noticed Tony's attitude subtly start to change. My doubts about myself seemed to be rubbing off on him. It was as though my lack of self-confidence undermined his confidence about his choice of me as his mate.

I guess my confidence in myself and my certainty that I was the right woman for Tony were stronger than my insecurities, because suddenly something clicked, and I saw that there was nothing to be worried about. After all, I was the one he had come home to.

I said in a carefree way, "Well, of course, she might have a better body than I do, but no one is better for you than me." He brightened. Whereas my doubts about myself had made him start to feel unsure, my confidence in myself made him feel good about being with me.

Knowing that it is important to value and love yourself, however, doesn't automatically make you do so. How, then, do you raise your self-esteem?

For some people, low self-esteem is a function of deeply rooted, systemic problems that are not likely to be resolved without the help of a skilled therapist. For many others, low self-esteem is due, in large part, to bad mental habits that can be overcome through awareness and discipline.

Many of us were taught as children that it is not polite to speak highly of ourselves. We got into the habit of putting ourselves down and magnifying our faults, paying a lot more attention to our flaws and the things we don't like about ourselves than to the things that make us feel good about ourselves. Focusing attention on something tends to strengthen and reinforce it.

Recognizing your own worth and value is not the same as being conceited. Putting yourself down is not the same as being humble and modest. Do you constantly make negative pronouncements about yourself, such as, "I have no discipline," "I'm too indecisive," "I hate my voice," and so forth? When you make a mistake, do you say, "I'm so dumb," "I have the worst memory," "I always put my foot in my mouth." Even when you do acknowledge a strength, are you quick to point to the flip side? "I'm creative. That must be why I'm so unorganized."

OK, you are not perfect. But must you keep dwelling on your imperfections? Even if you don't voice these insecurities, your internal dialogue reinforces them and creates a sense of low self-esteem, which comes across to others. If you had a friend who was as critical of you as you are of yourself, you would have broken off the friendship long ago. You wouldn't want to be around someone who constantly pointed out your shortcomings; yet that's what you do to yourself. Instead of empowering your faults by constantly focusing attention on them, why not emphasize your strengths? I don't mean that you should walk around saying how great you are. Again, it is what you say to yourself that matters most.

If you think you seriously lack self-esteem, you can go into therapy and work on yourself, but for most of us, a simple thing to do is to just start spending time every day writing down what is great about you. If you keep it up, you will be surprised by what you start to notice, and you can then begin to expand and develop those qualities.

By paying attention to what you think and say about yourself, you convert self-defeating mental habits into self-constructive ones. You are going to need to monitor your thoughts to make sure that your habit of putting yourself down doesn't creep back in when you are not paying attention. A lifelong habit is not broken overnight. It will take discipline and work, but the results will be well worth it.

Be Passionate

The second key to being attractive is being passionate about your life. It is clear why this is so important to the secret of being who you have always wanted to be. Who doesn't have

the vision, the goal, or the desire to live a full and passionate life? Who wouldn't want to see herself this way?

I have noticed that some people are merely going
through the motions, making a living, doing what they
have to do, and not having fun anymore. For these people,
finding a relationship is just another burden or item on
their "to-do" list. Being with such a person is, as you can
imagine, a turnoff and a drag. Who wants to be someone's
obligation, project, or goal?

If you are attractive, you have a life someone else would
be interested in being part of because you are so turned on
by it. You and the other person don't necessarily have to
have shared interests or even enjoy doing the same things.
It is not like the personal ads: "Must like biking, hiking in
the woods, sitting by the fire, and classical music." That is
not what makes a relationship. You don't have to be excited
about the same things, but you do need to be excited about
the person you are with.

You need to bring passion to a relationship. A relationship doesn't give it to you. I repeat, people want to be
around someone who is turned on by what he or she is
doing—and that includes work. Not every part of any job is
going to be exciting and wonderful, but at least some part of
it is. And if it is not, if you are not being nurtured and
turned on by your work, get another job. There are other
jobs out there. Because you can't deaden yourself all day
long, five days a week, and come home and expect someone
to make you feel alive again or to want to be with you.

You also can't afford to postpone living. You can't wait to

do certain things until you are in a relationship. For example, you really love to travel, but you are not going to travel alone. When you have a relationship, then you will travel. Or you want a house and love remodeling, decorating, and entertaining, but you are not going to do any of that until you get married. Now you are not only putting off doing those things; you are putting off doing the very things that make you excited about getting up in the morning. More important, you are putting off living. In other words, you are a little dead—or at least not fully alive—which is not a major turn-on for most men.

We all like being with someone who is happy rather than someone who is cynical, whiny, grumpy, or hard to please. This was really brought home to me when I was in Los Angeles with my friend Sarah. Sarah is a large woman, and although she is very pretty, you wouldn't consider her a knockout—especially in a city known for its worship of anorexic-looking bodies. When we started our trip, had you asked me which of us was better looking, I would have said (modestly) that I was. I was certainly thinner than she. But by the end of three days, I felt like chopped liver.

Men would literally stop Sarah on the street. They fawned over her in restaurants and stores, barely noticing me. After a while, I realized they were attracted to the same thing I love about her. She is a happy, sparkling person who exudes joie de vivre. She is fun to be with, and she is always laughing. She is not uptight about her size. She carries herself with confidence, obviously comfortable with herself just the way she is. Men trip over themselves to be around her.

We are attracted to people who have fun, who enjoy themselves, and who appreciate life. That is also, in our heart of hearts, who we want to be.

Keep Up Appearances

There are qualities that shine from the inside out, and there are qualities that shine from the outside in. How you look is very important to being attractive. We all share a visual appreciation for beauty, and men especially are visual animals, so how a woman looks is critical to attracting their attention and interest.

Some time ago, someone made the judgment that the way a person looks is superficial; therefore, it should not affect our judgment of him or her, which should always be based on deeper human qualities. To care about someone else's looks is shallow; to care about your own is vain. Yet we all care about such things, and we often feel guilty about it.

To exercise some visual discrimination in other areas of our lives, however, is not considered shallow or base. To be enchanted by a sunset or a field of wildflowers is akin to spirituality; to appreciate great art is noble. Yet these things engage the same sense of sight as looking at another human. Most of us like to look at something that pleases us, just as we like to smell, taste, and feel that which makes us feel better. It enhances the pleasure of being with them. So why is it so wrong to be attracted to someone who looks good, and what is so awful about wanting to look good for another? Be honest, whom would *you* prefer to look at across a dinner table, Brad Pitt or Rodney Dangerfield? And men are much more adamant about this than women.

When people come to my home for dinner, I want it to be a pleasant experience for them. I make sure that the house is clean and that there are flowers on the table or something good-smelling cooking in the oven. I want them to feel honored. Now, do I worry about what they will think of me, of my housekeeping, my taste in furnishings? Sure, I admit I want to impress them, and I worry how they will judge me. But even this worry is a sign of respect for the guests, that I care what they think of me.

The truth is that in order to have the greatest advantage in finding a relationship, a woman needs to be attractive. Nowadays, men don't have to put up with an unattractive woman. You don't want to lower your standards in a mate; why should they? A great guy deserves to have it all, as do you.

If I set aside all other factors involved in a woman's personality, the first thing that attracts a man to a woman is her looks. And for the most part, the better looking a woman is, the more men she will attract and the better the quality of those men will be. For women, the initial chemistry that makes a man attractive is his power—which can be expressed by being successful, rich, or accomplished. There are exceptions to what causes this initial chemistry, but not many. (I explain this in more detail in Chapter 7.)

Just as most women will be turned off by an unemployed, poor, and unaccomplished man, even if he is very hot-looking, a man is turned off by an unattractive, overweight woman even if she is very accomplished and financially independent. Likewise, most men are very happy with a gorgeous woman who has not been successful in a career. And women seem to find men who are not tops in the looks department but are rich, famous, or incredibly talented.

It may not be popular or politically correct to say so, but men care about what a woman looks like—and they care a lot! You may be the greatest, kindest, most fun woman around, but no man is going to find out about all your wonderful qualities unless he is attracted enough by your appearance to meet and get to know you. In an ideal world, it wouldn't be this way, but in case you haven't noticed, we are living in a less than ideal world, and it is the only one we've got.

Many women think that being attractive is something reserved for twenty-year-olds and Sophia Loren. Those women are going to have to resign themselves to being single or hope to find someone who sees the "deeper" beauty within them. The rest of us would like to have our pick of men. You and I want the real gold, not the consolation prize. And I say you can get it.

By doing certain things about how you look, you can make a huge difference in how you feel about yourself. It doesn't change who you are, but it does make a big difference when you feel great about yourself. If you feel good about who you are and the way you look, if you meet your own standards, you won't sell yourself short and will naturally demand someone who also meets your standards.

As I keep saying, the better you feel about yourself, the

greater your advantage. You want someone who could have anyone but chooses you. You are not going to feel good if the reason he is with you is because you're the best he could get.

By now, you are saying you don't want to be loved just for your appearance. Don't worry; you won't be. Remember, no matter how gorgeous you are, if you don't have other wonderful qualities, no one worth loving will waste his time with you.

Get Thee to a Beauty Parlor

Today, there is no excuse for not looking good. I know you claim to dress for yourself and look good for yourself, but the truth is, you don't have to look at yourself. Other people have to look at you. And you must admit that you like it when a guy looks good. It is enjoyable. I don't care if he is doing it for himself or not. But I am especially flattered if he looks good for me.

It pays big dividends to care about your looks and do something about your appearance. As we get older, it takes more effort to look good than when we were younger. I am all for natural beauty, but even those of us who looked beautiful without makeup when we were thirty usually need some by the time we are fifty. Our skin tone often changes; our eyes fade. I never used to put liner on my eyes. Now I don't leave the house without it—not so that I have a "made-up" look, but so that my face is seen rather than disappearing into a drab and tired look. I don't feel tired and drab. Why should I look it?

If you have any doubt about how to use makeup effectively, have it done once by someone who can give you a makeup lesson. Most cosmetic counters have certain days each month when they do free makeovers and teach you how to do it. You can learn how to put on your own makeup so it works for you.

Hair tends to lose its shine with age. And very few women gray well. Why should we put up with such indignities? Even if gray hair looks good with your skin tone, it still needs to be brightened and conditioned. If gray doesn't suit you, then put a rinse on it, put in some highlights, do something! The first time, you may want to go to a professional, someone who really knows what he or she is doing with your hair. And if you can do it yourself afterward, fine, but at least figure out how to have it done so your hair looks classy and beautiful.

And remember to have your makeup and hair updated every once in a while. You can't wear the same look at every stage of your life. Many women get stuck in a style from the past that doesn't fare well in the present. Nothing looks older than a fifty-year-old trying to look like a twenty-year-old. It is not that you have to be trendy, but you do need to be current and show a sense of style. Yes, it should be your style, but it should be your style in the present, not your style of twenty years ago. If your response is, "I can't be bothered," you are being just like the person who can't be bothered to tidy up the house before the guests arrive. Or you say, "It's not natural!" Well, I say you can't afford such trivial luxuries. It is not natural to paint your house either, and still you find the money and a way to do it. You want to protect your investment. What bigger investment do you have in your life than maintaining your love and passion?

Dress for Success

Clothes can make a huge difference, either positive or negative, in your appearance. You don't have to spend a fortune or have a huge wardrobe to be well dressed. But you do have to put in some time and thought.

Most people are in one of three places about clothes: (1) they have good taste and dress well; (2) they have good taste and don't dress well; (3) they don't have good taste and don't dress well.

If you are in the first group, no action is needed: keep doing what you are doing. If you are in the second group, you probably don't know how to look at yourself objectively or are stuck in a style that worked for you in the past but doesn't now. A petite, perky woman who dresses as if she were tall and elegant or a woman wearing the same hairstyle she wore twenty years ago in college are examples of people in this category. If you are in this group, you should get some help in order to see yourself better. All you probably need is a little jump start, and you will be fine on your own.

In my experience, people in the third group can be either

the easiest or the most difficult to work with. The important thing is to admit you don't know how to dress. Big deal. No one is good at everything, and the things you are good at are probably much more important. What you need to do is hire or ask someone to help you look your best. Be committed to looking good, not to proving you have a flair for dressing.

Wearing clothes in which you do not feel attractive diminishes your self-esteem. If you are like most people, you are happy with only about half the clothes in your closet. The remaining items are "things that might come back into style," "bargains," and the forty-three old shirts you are keeping to wear next time you garden. Each time you bought a pair of pants, a sweater, or a skirt on sale, you probably said, "For $30, I can't go wrong." But guess what. You have gone wrong twenty times for $30.

It is time to clear out everything in your closet that does not help you look and feel your best. And like most people, you will probably need help on this one. Remember, you are the one who got yourself into this mess in the first place. Pick someone who will be ruthless in forcing you to get rid of anything that doesn't make you look your best.

Consider Nips and Tucks

While it is politically correct to berate the idea of plastic surgery as vain, wrong, and ugly, the number of these surgeries is increasing steadily. Though few people want to admit they would even consider such an indulgence, many are going under the knife.

We are not supposed to talk about plastic surgery, and goodness knows, we know better than to ever recommend to someone that perhaps it is something he or she should consider. So I am daring to tread where many won't—at least publicly. As I have said throughout this chapter, looking the best you can is only to your advantage in finding a relationship. And with what is now available through plastic surgery, no one has to settle in the looks department. Just as we have accepted contact lenses or wearing braces as normal, the little "corrections" done through surgery are becoming more and more available and affordable to those of us who are not rich.

The secret of this book is being the person you have always wanted to be—and that includes how you look. Very few of us dream of having a "wattle" under the chin or a roll around the midriff. What I want to tell you is, there are certain things about aging you have to put up with, but how you look isn't one of them! I want to give you permission to explore the options. Believe me, you will not be alone. Thousands of people are having these procedures done; they just aren't talking about it.

Plastic surgery can do a lot for you in terms of feeling good about yourself and being more attractive. Some people argue that it is natural to age, and we should accept it rather than take action as drastic as plastic surgery. My response to this is one I mentioned earlier in this chapter: it is natural for shoes to wear out, too, but we generally don't like the way they look with holes in them, so we get them fixed or get new ones.

Now, if you really like the look of the worn-out shoes, that is a different story. A friend who is fifty-four and thinking of what she would like to change—getting her neck tightened and some collagen put in the creases in her face—told me, "I love my 'crinkles' around my eyes. They've come from all the laughing and happiness in my life, and I would never get rid of them. I think they're beautiful."

Some overweight women think and feel they are beautiful just as they are. So I repeat, if you feel beautiful the way you are, then you are beautiful, and don't you dare change anything.

Several times when I have mentioned to friends that I was considering a face-lift, the argument has been, how could I do it when I could end up looking like some television personalities whose face-lifts have left them looking perpetually surprised? But there are thousands of people we see every day, and we have no idea they had face-lifts, because they had good surgeons and they look natural. We simply think they look young for their age.

Take a really honest look at yourself. We are so used to seeing ourselves that we don't see the changes that have slowly taken place. Again, I don't think that if you are sixty years old, you should look like a twenty-year-old. I think you should look like a really great sixty-year-old. Or why not look as if you were forty if you are fifty or sixty?

If, every time you look in the mirror, you are patting your

chin or stretching your cheeks to see what a face-lift might offer you, then at least go talk to a plastic surgeon. If you have any idea that plastic surgery might be helpful to your looks and how you feel about your looks, take the time to get more information. It will not cost you anything to get a consultation with a good plastic surgeon.

Most surgeons can even provide a computer enhancement so you can see what it would look like if you had the surgery. Plastic surgery is not as prohibitively costly as many people think, and most plastic surgeons now have payment plans that help make it more affordable. There are also a lot of simple things you can do to correct droopy eyelids, bags under your eyes, a sagging neck. These smaller, less expensive operations can make a big difference in how you look in the mirror, how you look to others, and how you feel about yourself.

I mentioned earlier in this chapter that getting your teeth fixed—whether with braces, bonding, or whitening— is fairly common in our society now. Only the very poor do not automatically have their children's teeth straightened. There are many adults, however, who did not get this done as children because it was then a luxury their families could not afford.

You may be fifty years old and have learned to live with crooked or yellow teeth, so it may seem stupid to do something about it now. I say, if it is something that bothers you, or if it takes away from your appearance, then it is definitely not too late to do something. My friend Leslie got braces at age fifty-two. She was embarrassed about them for a few days, but she told me how excited she was to do it after having been self-conscious about her teeth for as long as she could remember. Three weeks after she got the braces off, I saw her, and she looked amazing. I asked her what was different, and she said, "I'm smiling. You've never seen me with a full smile before."

Later in the chapter, I talk about how important your smile is in the game of attraction. Make sure you take good care of this asset, and by all means, do what you need to do so you can make full use of it. We expect to live long, long lives, so giving up on your looks at fifty or fifty-five is way too premature.

Thin Is In

We need to talk about being overweight. This is a big issue. Both men and women in our society are obsessed with weight, and interestingly, both men and women are obsessed with women's weight. If you look at the personal ads, the most frequent item in men's requests is that the woman be slim. (Women don't tend to place such great emphasis on weight in their ads for men.)

There are hundreds of books about weight and diet, including several taking the stance that women's desire to be thin is a conspiracy by men to keep their domination over women. There are other political theories in the battle of weight and the sexes; I have no problem with any of them. As a person who has always struggled with my weight, I wish my body size and shape (rather than Gwyneth Paltrow's) could be the ideal. But I have found it works better to deal with reality—and the reality is that not only do most men find a slim figure more attractive, but I do, too. I admit I have probably been brainwashed by films, magazines, and television into believing this, but the damage has been done. I feel better, and I sure think I look better, when I am thin.

I have also learned that, for most overweight people, being thin is not so easily accomplished. There are often deep psychological issues involved. What's worse is, there is not much compassion or understanding about this problem. Naturally thin people have little or no patience with someone overweight: "It's simple. You just eat less and exercise more." If it were this simple, however, we wouldn't see a new diet book on the best-seller list every month—not to mention the diet centers, exercise gurus, and countless infomercials.

Weight is an easy issue for women to whine about and use as an excuse for not having the relationship they want. "I'm too fat. Men only want skinny women." I have two responses to this. My first response is, "Lose weight." Maybe so far nothing has worked for you, but just as you shouldn't give up looking for a relationship, you also shouldn't give up on something that can be so important to your health and your chances of having the relationship you want.

My second response—and perhaps, in many cases, the healthier one—is to accept who you are and find a man who loves "fleshy, voluptuous" women. They are out there. A woman came up to me at a seminar in New York. She asked me what I thought of Goddess Clubs. I told her I had never heard of them. She said Goddess Clubs are where men who love and worship overweight women go to meet them! I think this sounds great, especially if the overweight women feel like goddesses. If you love the way you look and feel, then certainly, you don't want to change it to find a relationship. What you want is to find someone who feels that way about you also.

You can get very cynical about this beauty thing. "Well, I could be beautiful, but I would probably be boring and mean." Or "Sure, if all I did was take care of my looks, I could look great, but my career and family would probably go down the drain." Or we put down someone who is beautiful or thin to justify our not being that way. "Oh, she's thin all right, but it's because she smokes." Or, "Of course, she looks good. All she has to do all day is go to aerobics classes and get her nails done."

But this business of accepting yourself first is vital to being successful. Because if you don't consider yourself beautiful and sexy, even if a man does, you will sabotage the relationship. You will put him down for liking you, he will lose your respect, and so there will be no chance of developing a truly loving, lasting relationship.

Caring about your appearance and about how you look honors those around you. Of course, if all you care about—or if all he cares about—is your looks, then we are talking about a shallow person at best. Wanting to be with someone attractive, however, is normal. And like it or not, it is here to stay.

You Are Never Fully Dressed without a Smile

You need to smile. In fact, I recommend that you smile—at the very least—at fifty men a week. You don't see fifty men a week? That is why I say you have to get out and socialize. "But they'll think I'm coming on to them!" You are. This is the point. Now, I am not saying you should go down to the docks at 2:30 A.M. and start smiling at the sailors. But in your daily life, when you are standing in line at the bank or post office, going up in the elevator to your doctor's appointment, waiting for your latte to be made at Starbucks, picking up your dry cleaning, looking for a video—smile and say hello. This isn't just a secret: this works like magic.

A smile not only does wonders for your appearance; it also communicates to another person that you are gracious, friendly, and approachable. Just as important, it communicates those same things to you.

I first discovered this when I was working as a waitress many years ago. The manager of the restaurant told me to start smiling at people. I protested that it would be phony to smile when I didn't feel like it. He said he didn't care if it was phony; he wanted me to smile. Not wanting to lose the job, I gave it a shot.

At first, I did have to fake it; my smiles were artificial.

But after I received a few genuine smiles in response to my fake ones, I started to actually feel happier and more friendly, and my smiles became more spontaneous. The more I smiled, the better time I had, and the more genuine my smiles became. And later, when I counted my tips and discovered they were about 20 percent higher than average, I burst out laughing.

The reason smiling works is that everyone out there is worrying about or trying to avoid rejection. I know you think you are the only one, but you are not. When you smile at a man, he thinks that he is not being rejected, so he comes right over to you. It works like radar. Everyone thinks men only go up to the most beautiful women, but that isn't true. They are usually terrified of going up to a gorgeous woman. So the more beautiful or striking you are, the more you need to smile.

Many gorgeous women, even some models, have come up to me to say that they never get asked out. They think it is because men believe they are stuck-up or arrogant, but, they tell me, "The truth is that I'm just painfully shy." I tell these women, smile and the men will not think you are a snob. "But I can't. I'm too shy!" Well, it has been physiologically proved that shy people can smile. So you don't have to go through six years of therapy to get over your shyness before you can meet a man. Personally, I like a shy personality, and nothing is more charming than a shy smile. So you don't have to change a thing—all you have to do is smile!

One night, when I was still single, I was in a bar in Seattle. The whole Seattle SuperSonics basketball team walked in. We didn't have movie stars in Seattle, so the athletes were the stars, and these guys were my type. Following my own advice, I smiled at one of the players. He was blond, blue-eyed, six feet eleven inches, and I had just read that he had signed a multimillion-dollar contract. My type to a T. Well, I must not have smiled high enough, because my smile got intercepted by the guy next to him, who was only six feet three inches, and he came over to me. My bad aim landed me my husband, Tony.

People who know us have a hard time believing that Tony, who is rather shy and reserved, came up to me in a bar. It just doesn't compute, but the reason Tony had the confidence to approach me is because he *thought* I was smiling at him!

A friend first heard me recommend smiling when she saw me on a local television show in New York City. While she thought it would be crazy to try it on the streets of New York, later that day, as she was running errands, she made a point of just *thinking* about smiling at the strangers she passed—and to her shock, most of them smiled at her and said hello! Of course, not everyone will make eye contact and return your smiles. That is OK. The point is not to *get* fifty smiles, but to *give* them.

Another woman, named Carol, approached me one night in Cleveland, where I was leading my seminar. She said she was a doctor and made a lot of money. She drove an expensive car and wore expensive clothes. She said men either were intimidated by her or wanted her for her money. She was sick of this and didn't think she should have to hide her success to find a relationship.

I said I was sure she was justified in everything she said and asked if I could share an observation. I told her that she came across as critical, cynical, and angry, and I thought that might be the problem. I suggested that smiling a lot might help her change her demeanor.

She was taken aback, but what I said sank in. She had been told once before that she had a chip on her shoulder about men, and she wanted to change that. When she returned the following week, she was much softer. She said that she felt less uptight and her friends had noticed a change in her as well. She also thought that men were responding to her differently.

You will probably find yourself becoming a friendlier, more open, and more cheerful person as a result of smiling at people, but that is only a side benefit. The main reason for doing it is that when you smile at people, you make it much easier for them to start a conversation with you, and in fact, more of them do so.

I know a lot of couples who first got together because one of them smiled. One woman who took my course in Seattle woke up on a Sunday realizing she had forty smiles left to give before the course session the next night. She positioned herself at the finish line of the Seattle Marathon and smiled at the runners as they finished the race. (Besides

being an efficient way to complete the assignment, it alle-
viated her concerns about safety, since she figured someone
finishing a marathon would not be likely to hassle her.)

To her delight, both men and women came up to thank
her for being there and tell her how encouraging and supportive her smiles were. She not only exceeded her quota of
fifty smiles; she later ended up marrying one of the runners
she met that day!

get out and date

Don't worry. I am not going to try to convince you that dating is fun. I know how horrible it can be. I also know it works. Dating is a numbers game that leads to relationships: the more people you go out with, the greater your chances of finding someone with whom you really connect.

The advice, rules, dos, and don'ts in this chapter are based on my experiences with thousands of single people of all ages. This is a dating survival guide that will allow you to avoid their mistakes and move from dating to a relationship with as little wear and tear as possible.

I: Just Do It

If your goal were to become vice president of your company, you wouldn't say, "No way I'm going anywhere near a client meeting," or "I refuse to meet with the sales team." If you planned on becoming a concert pianist, you wouldn't say, "I don't have time to practice," or "I won't play scales." If you wanted to be an Olympic swimmer, you wouldn't say, "I don't want to get my hair wet."

But you, a single person whose goal is to be in a relationship, say things like, "I want a relationship, but I don't like the dating scene." If I knew exactly when and where you would meet the person who is perfect for you, we would have charged a lot more for this book. There is no way around it: you are going to have to bite the bullet and go on dates. A lot of dates.

Women say to me, "All the guys I've gone out with are either emotionally unavailable or they are jerks." I ask them, "How many dates have you had in the last year?" They reply, "Two." I say that is an insufficient number of dates to pronounce such a sweeping judgment. Salespeople know that not every prospect turns into a customer, so they call on prospect after prospect. They consider themselves successful if one out of every dozen signs an order.

As I said in Chapter 4, you should be picky. So you are going to have to go through a lot of men to have your pick. Fortunately, there are a variety of resources—including personal ads, dating services, and your personal network—to help you in your quest for people to date. Later in this chapter, there are tips for making the most of these resources.

2: Don't Be a Snob

People always tell me they know they would never be interested in someone who would hang out at a bar, join a dating service, or go on a blind date. I tell them they have no idea. Dating is not about limiting options but expanding them.

Two of the biggest mistakes you can make in looking for a relationship are thinking you know which people are your "type" and thinking you know where you will meet them. (The myth that you know your type is so disastrous that I have devoted an entire chapter to it.)

3: Don't Whine about Time

Even very busy people make time for those things that matter most to them. Finding a life mate is a high-priority project. It is going to take the kind of time you would expect to spend on something this important.

On an episode of the television program *Ally McBeal*, Ally is justifying to her roommate taking action to find love: "We are two women who work twelve hours a day at our jobs. We admit that our personal lives are more important than our jobs, yet we do nothing, put no effort and not a fraction of the time into making a personal life."

Besides, when you are in a relationship, you will want to spend time with your mate. Get into the habit of making time for a relationship now.

4: Lighten Up

When you were nineteen, you didn't have to be convinced that someone would make a perfect spouse before you would go out for coffee with him. When you got older, you started to take dating far too seriously. You started to confuse going to dinner with signing mortgage papers.

My friend Carol told me about a guy named Steve who called her recently because a friend had given him her number. During their initial phone conversation, he told her, "I'm a doctor; I'm finishing my residency. When I finish, I'm moving to Israel. Anyone I'm with has to be Jewish or convert to Judaism, keep a kosher house, and raise our children according to Jewish law." She said, "And I was thinking maybe we'd go to a movie."

The time for determining whether someone is a suitable life mate is after you date, not before. That is what dating is for.

5: Socialize

As I said earlier, the reason relationships seemed to happen so spontaneously in school is that you were socializing all the time. Then you got older and began spending most of your time at work, where, unlike the student union, most people are not single, available, and cute.

I used to encourage people to date coworkers, but now that male/female relationships in the workplace have become so politicized, I advise caution. If you are not in danger of violating any company policies and you are being appropriate to the work environment, then you may find the office a good place to network with members of the opposite sex.

The best way to meet people is to do things you like to do, things that are related to your interests. If you are interested in opera, instead of sitting at home listening to CDs, start attending the opera, go to discussion groups about opera, join a guild to raise money for your local opera, and so on. I also recommend choosing activities at which you are more likely to meet men. For example, I wouldn't take up knitting to meet men, but I would look at taking up golf or skeet shooting or fly-fishing. "Well," you say, "I'm not going to lie and pretend I like something just to meet a man. After we're married, he'll expect me to go bowling every Tuesday night!"

Lying and deceit have no place in a relationship, so don't do things you know you hate. It is a plus, however, to be open to new things. Trying something new is energizing and keeps you young; having new interests is exciting and refreshing. Many women who have tried new things to meet men have in the process found a new hobby or passion. One friend took up skeet shooting, found a man, and also found a wonderful hobby—closer, actually, to a new addiction—and a whole new group of friends. She is not only in love; she is totally turned on by her sport as well.

Wanting to meet men is sufficient reason in itself to do something. We never thought there was anything wrong in joining a sorority to establish a social life in college or attending football games. (I never missed a game; I also never watched one.) If you can get over the idea that there is something wrong with you for wanting a relationship—and goodness knows, you should have gotten over that in the earlier chapters of this book—then you can let go of any shame about going places specifically to meet new men.

So end all the covert operations and start a fresh and open campaign to meet potential men. Make sure all your friends are looking out for you, not only for dates to fix you up with but also for any activities they know of that you should attend: lectures at their place of business, after-hours business get-togethers, community meetings.

These are all great places to get involved and get active. And you don't have to worry about whether everyone is single or not, because if you get involved with new people, they have single friends. Remember, 40 percent of the adult population is single, so just get out there and you will meet them.

Now if you can't handle this dating thing and going out to meet men, and you are certain you are too shy or too vulnerable or too fragile, then there is one thing left for you to do—*pray!* And if this is what you resort to, then at least go to your church or synagogue to do this praying.

6: Be Personal

Once you meet people, it is important to actually get to know them, which is not the same as spending time with them. Small talk is fun and a good way to get familiar with someone's personality, but you should try to create an opening for deeper conversation as well.

This is another aspect of relationships we were much better at in school. In college, you could meet someone at a party and feel as if you were close friends by the next day. It wasn't unusual back then to stay up half the night with someone you had just met, getting to know each other. As you got older, you became more concerned with the outcome of relationships, with where they were going, and less interested in being with someone just for the sake of sharing experiences.

To get personal with someone, you have to learn how to become a great interviewer. Normally, when you interview people you have just met, you ask them what their job is, where they grew up, where they like to go skiing, what restaurants they enjoy, and so on. You discuss the wrapping and never get inside the package. Questions like these help you discover whether someone fits into your lifestyle, not what he is really like. The spirit in which you ask these questions is as important as the questions themselves. This is not about probing into people's private lives or interrogating them about how many kids they plan to have. You are not interviewing people for the job of "prospective spouse." You are just trying to get to know them.

If you are not really interested in someone, try pretending that you are. You may find that you actually do become interested. The key is to listen. And since it is a rare person whose favorite subject isn't him- or herself, don't be surprised if your interest in him makes your date think you are fascinating.

By getting personal with the people you date, you will help ensure that you don't let "the one" slip through your fingers. And when you do eliminate someone, your decision will be an informed one. You will know who it is you are passing up.

7: Don't Hunt in a Pack

Avoid going out with more than one friend; a pack of women tends to be intimidating. Better yet, go out by yourself. You will be more focused on meeting people and will seem more available and approachable. Also, you won't have to worry about someone else's opinions. It is hard enough to meet someone new without your friend saying, "How could you be interested in him?" or "I can't believe you flirted with every guy at the bar." If you do go out with a friend, be sure to make it clear that this outing is part of your project. Make sure he or she supports your goal of meeting people.

In Defense of Bars

Many women think, "Well, at my age, I can't go to a bar." But there are bars with an older and classier crowd if you are willing to risk looking for them, and the truth is, people go to bars specifically to meet people. That is why some people say, "I'm not going to go. It's a meat market." I have also had people say, "You can't meet men at a bar because everyone is an alcoholic," which is not true.

While you may find men who want to pick up someone for the night, that does not hold true for the majority. So bars can be a good place to meet men, but make sure you never leave a bar with someone you have just met. Get a phone number or arrange to meet in a neutral location until you know enough to be sure it is safe.

You may have to do some research to scope out which bars in your city are frequented by the kind of people you would like to meet. People who know us think it is funny I met my husband in a bar, because I don't drink. If you haven't been to any bars lately, you might be surprised at the number of soft drinks and bottled waters being consumed in many of them.

When you go to a bar (or anywhere else), be up-front with yourself about what you are doing there. I remember being asked on several occasions, "What's an intelligent, good-looking woman like you doing in a bar?" I would answer, "I'm here to meet someone. What are you doing here?"

8: Don't Ask Men Out

Most men don't respond well to a woman's asking them out. Even though many things about relationships have changed in recent years, there is still a courting etiquette that dictates that the man ask the woman out. Just as it would make most men uncomfortable if you went around opening doors for them, asking them out can get things off to an awkward start.

"But," women shout in protest, "that goes against everything you have said so far. Now not only do I have to wait and hope that some man discovers me but that the guy who does find me is someone I am interested in. I have no say in the matter at all."

Then there are the men who say they are the exception because they like women to ask them out. (Why do they like women to ask them out? So they can avoid rejection! Let women deal with being turned down for a while!) But these same men get very nervous and uncomfortable when a woman does ask them out. Somehow their masculinity is threatened. Their role in the courting ritual is no longer defined.

I suggest a method that will allow you to eat your cake and have it, too. Try saying to a man you are interested in, "I enjoyed talking to you [meeting you, getting to know you a little, bumping into you, and so on]. I'd really love it if you asked me out."

If all you get from this book is this one line and you use it, it will be worth much more than the price you paid. In fact, it will be worth more than all the books you have bought combined, because this line works like you won't believe.

It is so good, I am going to repeat it: "It's been lovely talking to you. I'd love for you to ask me out." With this line, the man gets what he wants: he is reasonably sure you are not rejecting him. It also allows you to select whom you are interested in and make something happen in getting a date.

This is not being aggressive and does not put a man off guard the way asking him for a date does. It is gracious and allows him to feel like a man and ask you out, and it allows you to feel like a woman being asked out on a date. It feels right and "comfortable" and alleviates all the awkwardness about who asked whom out, who pays, and so forth.

Now, if you have been seeing a man for a while and you want to ask him to go to a concert or a movie, fine, but I really suggest you wait a while.

I cannot stress enough how important it is to tell men that you want to go out with them. You have got to do this. If you notice, men are not asking women out. The reason for this is explained in more detail in Chapter 10, in which I talk about commitment. But the bottom line is that men's threshold for rejection was reached when they were about eighteen. So they are not going to ask you out unless they get the assurance that you will not be rejecting them.

You cannot be any more subtle than this. Just saying that you enjoyed meeting them will probably not work; even saying that you hope to see them again doesn't usually get through. I am serious here. I have asked hundreds of men about this. What you consider to be an obvious invitation is not obvious to them.

You may find this embarrassing at first, but you will be amazed at the results you will get. I offer you a money-back guarantee that this will work. The truth is, you need to start dating, and you need to start dating now. You are not going to read this book and have a relationship tomorrow; you have to do some dating in between. And this "line" will get you dates.

Of course, not every man you say it to will ask you out, but I promise if you say this to ten men a week, you will have a date every week. I know you aren't just looking for a date; you are looking for a real relationship. But in Chapter 7, you will learn that you can't tell right away who is going to end up as the real thing anyway. Besides, just being out there is going to get you into circulation, meeting men wherever you go.

A woman took my seminar in Vancouver, British Columbia. She wrote me three months after the seminar to tell me that, since the seminar, she has had more dates than she previously had altogether in her entire life. She also made the point in the letter that she was fifty-five years old. "I'm no little cutie in a miniskirt, and I'm getting more dates now than when I was!" What made the difference, she said, was telling men she would like them to ask her out. It made all the difference.

Keep doing this. After the first date, if you want a second date, make sure you say, in English (as opposed to body language or insinuation), that you had a lovely time and you hope he will ask you out again. I know this is ridiculous, but I also know what I am talking about. The men in my seminars always laugh at this part, because they, too, realize how thickheaded they are.

"I could never do that," you say. Then don't. I can't make you, but what have you tried that has worked? A woman in Washington, D.C., shot up at this point in the class to say, "I don't think we should have to do that." I agree, and while we are protesting, I want to add that we shouldn't get fat when we eat doughnuts and I should make a million dollars!

This advice goes against the counsel in the book *The*

Rules. First of all, let me say that what I like about that book is, it tells women to value themselves. This is the idea of "self-esteem" I talk about throughout this book. But I don't at all condone or recommend the manipulation and deception its authors advocate. I don't think you get an authentic, profound relationship—which is what I assume you are looking for—by trickery and playing games. That is demeaning and offensive to both you and the men with whom you do it.

My real gripe about their advice is that it doesn't work, especially with men in the after-forty age group, because they have so little tolerance for rejection. If a man calls you on Friday for a date on Saturday or Sunday, by *The Rules* you are supposed to refuse, even if you are free and would love to go out with him. I am telling you that if you follow that advice, nine times out of ten, you will never hear from that man again—not because he is not interested (of course, he was interested; he asked you out, for God's sake!) but because it was tough enough to ask in the first place. One rejection might set him back months in asking any woman out. And I am not just talking about wimpy men. In fact, it is often true that the more powerful and successful the man, the more he abhors failure or rejection.

That is why you have to let a man know not only that you would like to go out with him but that, if asked, you *will* go out with him. So if you are busy when he asks you out, then do not just say no. Say you would love to go out with him and even suggest an alternative time.

9: Offer to Pay on a Date

Do offer to pay for your dinner, drinks, movie ticket, and so forth when you go out on a date. Don't insist if the man declines your offer, but you will find that men really appreciate even the offer. Another way to reciprocate is to invite him over for dinner.

10: Do Date Defensively

Many women complain to me that, in this day and age, you don't know whom you are meeting out there. There are stalkers, mass murderers, and real psychos. I have heard more horror stories than I ever need to know.

No one, certainly not I, can argue with this fact. I look at dealing with the dangers of dating, however, in the same way I look at dealing with the dangers of driving. Nothing is more dangerous than driving. Traffic accidents and fatalities have skyrocketed and only seem to increase each year. Most of us are quite aware of the hazards, yet most of us keep driving and try to be careful and alert to the driving of others.

This same wariness and consciousness is called for in dating. The fact that dangers exist should not stop you from dating; it should just dictate that you exercise caution. Never go home with a man early on in a relationship. And if you don't know someone well, or were not introduced by someone who knows him well, meet in public places for your first few dates.

For Single Parents

Many single parents feel that dating is more difficult for them, and they are right. Each person you add to a relationship makes it more complicated and complex. Being a single parent, however, does not have to prevent you from finding a relationship.

Even though your children are your priority, you need to make time for yourself and for having a relationship. Besides, doing so will have a positive impact on your well-being, which can only benefit your children. I recommend that you set aside one night a week for this purpose. Stop using your kids as an excuse. Surely you can find someone to take care of them; we are only talking about one night a week.

Don't bring your children into the relationship until it is a relationship. Don't say, "I'm a package deal, so anyone who dates me has got to know my children and vice versa." I am not suggesting that you hide your children or lie about the fact that you are a parent, just that you establish your relationship before bringing them into it. In the beginning, a relationship is fragile. Only after you build a strong foundation—by getting to know each other and establishing intimacy and trust—can a relationship withstand the strain children tend to put on it.

But protecting the relationship is not the most important reason for this advice. It is not to your children's benefit to expose them to relationships that are not established and secure. If the relationship breaks up, the children will always lose. If your children like the person you are dating, it can engender hopes, expectation, and attachment, which can lead to feelings of loss and disappointment if you break up. If your children don't like the person you are dating, it can be a difficult and frustrating experience for them, one that you shouldn't put them through unnecessarily.

If You Date a Single Parent

Contrary to popular opinion, you don't have to like his children and they don't have to like you in order for the two of you to have a relationship. It may take time for your relationship with his kids to develop, and it may never be wonderful. Workable is sufficient.

It is important to be clear with his children (and with yourself) that you aren't trying to replace their mother. Also, don't try to parent another person's child and don't offer unsolicited advice about parenting, even if you think you know best. This is a real source of problems in many relationships. Stay out.

If you both have kids, things can definitely get complicated. There are professional counselors who specialize in dealing with the problems that frequently occur in "blended" families. If you are experiencing difficulties, don't wait to seek this kind of help. By getting support earlier rather than later, you can learn skills that will help you get past the challenges and prevent a lot of pain.

Dating Resources

In most cities, personal ads, on-line networking, dating services, and singles groups, clubs, and events abound. As with most other things, what you get out of these resources will depend on what you put into them. Just joining an organization or placing an ad isn't enough; you have to actually show up for events and make an effort to meet the people who are there.

And remember, the purpose of these resources is to create a flow of new people into your life, not to qualify and screen them.

Personal Ads

Start by selecting one or more publications for your ad. You can approach this as though you were a business advertiser and find out from various publications what their demographics are or just choose a newspaper or magazine you like to read. It is a good idea to read a bunch of ads to get a feel for them. Notice the length, content, and style of those you like and use them as a guide when you write your own.

The biggest mistake people make in writing personal ads is listing too many criteria designed to screen people out. It is fine to mention some things you are looking for, but don't overdo it. The goal is to generate the maximum number of new prospects. The time to screen for quality is after you meet the respondents, not before.

The key to handling the responses to your ad is to answer all of them (with the exception of those from obvious creeps). Sally did not have the benefit of this advice when she placed her personal ad, a few weeks before she took my seminar. She separated her forty-five responses into a "good" pile and a "reject" pile. Seven men made it into the good pile; there were thirty-eight rejects. She began phoning the good ones. The first got disqualified on the telephone, and the second rejected her after three promising dates. After this rejection, she didn't feel like calling anyone else.

During my seminar, Sally realized she had been overdoing it a bit with the criteria she was using to screen men out. She saw that she had not given the respondents enough of a chance. So she went through her two piles again. This time, only three responses landed in the reject stack. She began calling the remaining respondents one by one until, midway through the pile, she met a man she really liked. She ended up marrying him later that year. They still laugh about the fact that he was originally "reject number 19."

Whether you answer an ad or someone answers yours, one thing to avoid is an extended initial telephone conversation. After talking with someone for three hours on the phone, it can feel anticlimactic when you meet for a date. Try not to stay on the phone for more than ten or fifteen minutes.

If you have a positive reaction to someone on the phone, see whether you can arrange a time and place to meet. It is usually best to meet at a public place like a coffeehouse, restaurant, or park. While I like the idea of men picking women up at their home when you go on a date, I don't advise this for the first time you meet someone from an ad.

On-Line Networking

Meeting people on the Internet is fun. This is a growing way for people to meet other people and can be very effective if done right. There are now lots of local bulletin boards, chat lines, and user groups that provide a "place" where you can connect to other singles with Internet access. It may be impractical for some people because of geographic considerations, but it is worth exploring.

Try logging on at different times of the day and week. Once you have connected with someone you find interesting, don't wait too long to meet him in person. Otherwise, you can end up investing a lot of time and energy in what amounts to an imaginary relationship when you should be getting involved with flesh-and-blood people.

Katie called me brimming over with happiness. She couldn't wait to tell me she was "in a relationship." I was beyond thrilled for her. She was a talented, vivacious artist but was quite a bit overweight, and up to now, had experienced a lot of failure in finding a relationship. "Tell me everything about him. How did you meet?" "On the Internet. He lives in Montana, and we have so much in common. We love talking to each other. He's so kind."

My stomach dropped as I anticipated the answer to the next question. "Have you met?" "No, but we will soon. I'm waiting until I lose weight." As gently as I could, I told her it was fine to continue the communication with this guy, but it wasn't a relationship until they had at least met. In truth, it was a fantasy. He was a pen pal, which is fine unless it becomes an excuse to avoid or postpone a real relationship. I wasn't even primarily worried that he would reject her when he saw her because of her weight, but that, in meeting and spending time with him, the fantasy bubble would burst.

That is just what happened. Amazingly, Katie did lose a lot of weight and hopped on a plane to Montana looking like a million bucks. They weren't together more than an hour before she realized she had made a horrible mistake. Even though she had talked to this guy for hours before they met and there had been warning signs, they were too easy to overlook when the two of them were not face-to-face.

Don't get me wrong. I know many couples who met on the Internet. I am just warning you that until you actually meet face-to-face, even if you have spent hours together online, it is only an introduction, not a relationship.

Dating Services

Many people come to my seminars complaining that they "tried a dating service" and didn't meet anyone. After a little probing, the truth always came out. They had submitted their video and waited for someone to discover them. This is like joining a gym and never going to work out, then complaining that it didn't help you get in shape. After my seminar, some of these same people went back to the service they had joined and got to work reviewing the videos of the other members and making contact with them. Of course, they got results.

Don't be put off by the high fees some dating services charge. It is usually possible to negotiate a lower fee. Try it. Remember, the purpose of these dating resources is to increase the flow of people into your life. Use them to connect with as many people as possible.

There are a lot of dating services available. Some are really fun and have great ideas. Some will suit your purpose better than others. There is a dating service called Just Lunch in many cities that offers an easy way to meet people. There is a coffeehouse called Common Grounds in New York City that runs a dating service right there. I have even heard of dry cleaners setting up bulletin boards for their customers who want to meet someone. So take the time to find out about what is available for you.

If Not Now, When?

This is the time you may be thinking, maybe you don't really want a relationship. It is looking like an awful lot of work, and you don't have the time or energy. After all, you are not so unhappy on your own, you have good friends, family, your career. Sound familiar? These are the thoughts that will lull you into inactivity. All I can say is that you may be OK for a while, but your real intentions will not go away. They will only turn into hard and bitter regret later.

Remember why you want a relationship and what you want from a relationship. It is also the time to call your support person and have him or her remind you and give you a good kick in the pants. Because the more you do and the sooner you do it, the sooner you will have a relationship. I know you don't want to settle, and I am telling you, you don't have to.

Dating, like the word *single*, generally implies an activity done by the young. Many women after forty assume they cannot go places to meet men because they risk looking foolish. They are right. But, then, when you go new places to see people you don't know, you risk looking foolish no matter what your age. The greater risk is that you will be judged and dismissed or rejected. As I said earlier, rejection is the greatest obstacle you need to overcome to find a relationship.

What motivated me to get out there was the realization that the risks were offset by the potential gains. If I didn't get out there, my chances of finding someone were pretty slim. I knew I wanted love and affection in my life, so I was willing to risk the embarrassment, humiliation, and rejection. And I honestly have to say, I experienced it all. It was horrible. I never got used to it. But boy, was it worth it!

Trains, Planes, and Automobiles (Places to Meet Men)

Attend sporting events:

Golf tournaments
Tennis matches
Basketball, baseball, or football games

Participate in athletic activities:

Softball
Volleyball
Aerobics or health club
Triathlon training club
Sailing or windsurfing
Jogging club
Martial arts
Skiing (especially with an organized ski club)
Horseback riding
Bicycling club
Tennis leagues (mixed doubles)
Hiking or mountaineering club
Swimming or scuba diving
River rafting
Dance classes (ballroom, country-western, salsa, tap)

Take a course, classes, or lessons in:

Boating
Art appreciation
Fly-fishing
Investments

Carpentry

Painting

Photography

Cooking

Language

Skeet shooting

Golf

Shop in:

Grocery stores, especially on "Singles Night" (if available)

Men's clothing stores

Auto supply stores

High-tech gadget stores like Sharper Image

Bookstores

Sporting goods stores

Computer stores

Wine shops

Camera shops

Hardware stores

Car dealerships

Attend cultural events:

Gallery openings

Plays (including the discussion groups)

Museums

Symphony or opera

Volunteer:

In a hospital
To help a political candidate
At a public television station
As a tour guide
In an art museum
To participate in a fund-raising event
To collect for a charity
For a tournament sport

Hang out at:

Racetracks
Marinas
Auctions
Libraries
Coffeehouses
Museums
Car washes

And:

Travel alone or go on a singles trip.
Go to bars during "happy hour."
Join or start a singles dinner group.
Eat breakfast out alone near business places.
Visit the zoo. (Many single parents are there with kids.)
Take a ferry ride.
Take your niece or nephew to the park.

Teach a class or workshop.

Go to trade shows.

Take up new hobbies (dog showing or bird-watching).

Walk in the park with your dog. (If you don't have a dog, borrow one.)

Join a choir or singing group.

Go to singles events.

Attend religious services.

Go to political events or party meetings.

Connect through local on-line singles bulletin boards.

Connect in line (at movies, grocery stores, banks, and so forth).

Go to car auctions.

Participate in car rallies.

Go to boat and auto shows.

you don't know jack about your type

The truth is, you don't know your type. And the fact that you don't know your type is not a problem. On the contrary, if you get anything out of this chapter, I hope it is a deep appreciation for the fact that you don't know your type. Because when you realize that, you can honestly say you are in the research and development stage: you are open to meeting all kinds of men, you are researching whom you are compatible with, whom you can feel close to and intimate with, who is fun, who makes you feel great, and who makes you feel awkward, ugly, or stupid. So not knowing your type is a good thing.

You, however, are certain you do know your type. You know whom you like; you know what kind of men appeal to you. You are not a kid; you have done the research; you have dated, had relationships, and *you are sure you know your type.* Now *that* is a problem. Because I want to point out to you where knowing your type has gotten you—here, alone, and reading this book.

The truth is, you have gone out with your type over and over again. You may even have married your type over and over again. And unless you are a widow who had a glorious, lasting relationship that only ended when your husband died, knowing your type has not turned out well for you. It has not led to a wonderful, nurturing, long-term relationship. Knowing your type—whom you have that special chemistry with, those feelings that tell you this is the one— is not working for you.

I think Jewish girls must be programmed by our parents to want to marry a doctor (a Jewish doctor, of course). There must be a device put in our cribs as babies that created this chemistry. All I know is that I rebelled against this parental pressure like crazy, was a hippie, got involved in radical politics, marched, protested, and didn't shave under my arms. And through it all, if a man said he was a doctor, or even in medical school, my heart fluttered and I was turned on. This still happens!

I must have dated enough doctors to staff a major hospital, but none of these dates ever turned into a long-term, great relationship; I am not saying that doctors stink in relationships; I am simply saying that my "type" is not my type!

The writer Rita Mae Brown defines insanity as doing the same thing over and over again and expecting a different result. I am not your therapist, but you might question whether this isn't what happens when you go after "your type" and let chemistry, feelings, and instinct be your guides and screening mechanisms.

But this situation gets a lot worse before it gets better.

Knowing your type is a very big problem, but it is not the biggest problem. The biggest problem is, you know who *is not* your type, and you know it within the first ten seconds of meeting someone. In fact, some of you are such quick studies that often you know even *before* you meet him. "Oh, he's a plumber [dentist, engineer, house painter]. He's not really my type." "He hunts [smokes, watches football, has children]? He's definitely not my type."

The single biggest mistake people make in looking for a relationship is screening people out too quickly based on the immediate chemistry or lack thereof.

Of course, human beings have always used "chemistry," that mysterious feeling that somehow is the indicator of whether this person is our soul mate or not, as a way to sort prospects and select a partner. I am going to demystify chemistry for you.

Men and women first began to live as couples, rather than simply coming together for sex, when we were still living in caves. The reason for this was survival, not love. As hunters and gatherers, they had to leave their caves to find food, but they also had offspring who, unlike most animals, required extended care. To survive as a species required collaboration. Men went out and got the food; women had babies and took care of them.

For a woman, choosing a partner was based on finding a good hunter, someone who brought home the prize of the hunt, not a measly rabbit. Her life and the lives of her children depended on the skills and accomplishments of this man. What the man looked for was a woman who was good breeding material. She was strong, healthy, and had the right size hips to squat and deliver a baby and still have dinner on the table that night—and her smell triggered his sexual interest.

So the bottom-line criteria for choosing mates were based on two things: rich (lots of food) and sexy. Interesting, isn't it? Especially when you look at how far we have come. And to this day, that is what chemistry consists of. Those feelings you get in the pit of your stomach are an instinct for survival that dates back to our cave-dwelling ancestors. It is an instinct that has served us well, since the species survived and flourished, but it had nothing to do with personality, spiritual connection, love, or intimacy.

The problem for us is not the instinct so much as how we interpret the chemistry we feel. If you have immediate chemistry with a man—you know, when your heart is racing, or you are flushed and excited—you interpret it as a sign that this is meant to be. You think it means this man is not only your type but most likely a candidate for the position of your designated soul mate as well. You think this chemistry is a very individual and personal phenomenon when in fact it is a prehistoric instinct for survival shared by all humans. It is as personal to you as getting up and walking on two feet is personal to you.

What if I told you I wanted to introduce you to a short man in his fifties with a big nose, thick glasses, and ears that stick out? Not your classic hunk. Sound interesting? What if I told you his name was Steven Spielberg? Notice a shift in attitude? In chemistry quotient?

Now I bring in a hunk: tall, gorgeous, classic, sexy. I introduce you to Frank, a male dancer who strips for a living. Not interested, right? No need for discussion; you know he is not your type. Might be OK for one night if you are really horny, but based purely on his "profession," you have ruled him out as a possible relationship.

Or what if I offer to introduce a guy to a real knockout— an exquisite woman with flawless skin, gorgeous hair, and a perfect body. Her name is Patti, and she sells doughnuts in the mall. "So?" he says, "she's employed; I'm no snob."

Really? Meet Rene, an extraordinary woman, a famous heart surgeon. People come from all over the world to study her surgical techniques. She is also an expert mountain climber, who has scaled all the major peaks in North America and others throughout the world. She is average-looking—not ugly, but she does have heavy calves and thighs. What? Not as interested?

For men, chemistry is still largely based on what a woman looks like; for women, it is still what a man does. The "rich man, sexy woman" syndrome remains intact despite thousands of years of history.

Everyone is pissed off about this. Women complain that men only care about the size of their breasts and their percentage of body fat. And men think that women only care about the size of their wallets.

Men have an unfair advantage in this chemistry business. I ask a man what does he do. He gets upset that all I care about is how much he makes. But I say, "You got to look at my breasts. I should be able to find out what you do." All men have to do is look to get their chemistry going. Women have to do paperwork. But being angry about chemistry is like being mad about the rain in Seattle. That is just the way it is.

This chemistry was viable for our mothers' generation and perhaps even for us until very recently. Most women needed a husband for financial security. Very few women worked outside the home, and it was considered a major hardship if a woman raising children worked or had a career. And a "good provider" was a good husband, *by definition*. It was honorable to support your wife and children, unlike today, when we demean this arrangement by calling him a "meal ticket."

Not so obvious was that a man also needed to be married, in that he needed a wife as an entrée into society. A man who was unmarried was not accepted, was suspect. He could not rise on the corporate ladder, could never run for political office. Not only did he need a wife, but she had to "look" the part. If his wife looked like a slob or acted like one, he missed the promotion. A wife could be either an asset or a liability to a man's career based solely on her outward demeanor.

It has only been recently that the reasons for mating have changed. For the most part, women don't need men to survive. And men no longer need a wife to ensure their career advancement. The functional requirements for mating have largely been supplanted by psychological or emotional needs. Now people are seeking a sense of security and belonging. They want intimacy, someone with whom to share their lives. We want deep, passionate relationships. We want someone we can talk to and with whom we can laugh and be intimate. Yet we keep going for people with whom we have chemistry or who fill the functional needs we no longer have.

It is chemistry that makes most of you decide if someone is or isn't "your type." There is nothing wrong with chemistry, but its value is limited. I think chemistry is great, but I think it is recreational. When I travel, I like to rent and watch movies in my hotel room. How I pick the movie is, any movie that stars Brad Pitt. The reason for this is not because they are great movies (unfortunately, his recent movies have been pretty lame) but because I have chemistry with Brad Pitt. This is my personal chemistry. I am sure you can't relate to it because it is a personal soul connection between me and Brad. And the reason I enjoy these movies is the chemistry.

So if you feel it, go ahead—enjoy it. Flirt all you want. But don't take it too seriously, and please don't use it as your only indicator of whether a relationship will succeed in the long run. An initially positive gut reaction doesn't mean you're going to have a good relationship with someone, nor does an initially neutral or even negative reaction mean you won't.

Any connection between your first reaction and what develops in a relationship is probably nothing more than coincidence. If you have ever been involved with someone with whom you had great chemistry only to find there was nothing to keep you together after the initial buzz wore off, you know what I am talking about.

What about "love at first sight"? Or your cousin Vera and her husband, who have a terrific marriage and knew right away that they were meant for each other? It is true; it happens.

Consider this: In my course, I give an assignment to interview two happily married couples about their relationships and specifically about their initial encounters. (The first challenge is to find two happily married couples.) So far, the participants have interviewed more than two thousand couples. I am not talking about two thousand couples who tolerate each other or stay together because it is comfortable. I am talking about two thousand couples in long-term, deeply passionate relationships. And guess what? When asked if they had any chemistry when they first met, 90 percent of these couples answered no!

So to use initial chemistry as your sole indicator of whether or not to have a cup of coffee with a man is ridiculous. Would you invest your money in a venture that had only a 10 percent chance of success?

Still, a lot of people can't resist a long shot. If they get that "magic feeling," they are off and running. It is not surprising. When you experience chemistry with someone, you like him right away. It is easy to connect. Flirting feels natural. You are eager to get to know him better. All you have to do is let nature take its course, and before you know it, you are "involved."

When there is no chemistry, it is a real "Catch-22." You are not motivated to get to know the person better, yet it is only by getting to know someone better that you will discover whether or not there is a real bond between you.

Does this mean you should avoid someone with whom you have initial chemistry? Absolutely not. If you feel an immediate spark, by all means, get to know him better. But you should also try to get to know men with whom you don't feel initial chemistry. By giving someone you don't think is your type a chance, you may discover that there is an attraction between you that is slower to build but every bit as passionate. This is the kind of chemistry that can last forever.

Beyond Chemical Dependency

In my seminars, I tell people to become "talent scouts." The job of a talent scout is to find a star before he or she has become one. There is no money in discovering somebody who has already been discovered. What you have been doing is going for the glitz, for people who are already shining. And you have probably found that they are already taken or that they don't live up to their initial promise.

Let's say you go to a party. There are ten available men there. Two of them are stars: they shine. Two of them are dogs: they bark. You approach the handsome ones, carefully avoiding the dogs. One of them snubs you; the other one leaves with a Christie Brinkley look-alike. Asked the next day how the party was, you say, "OK, but there was only one good man there, and he left before I had a chance to talk to him." I say there were six men there you never even saw. You see the stars, you see the dogs, but as for the others, unless their Dun & Bradstreet rating is being flashed in neon, you just walk by.

And I am talking real stars, real Tom Hanks–type stars, not a consolation star, not "Well, given how mediocre you are, this is the best you can expect." No, I am talking about gold, and you keep passing it by.

We have all had the experience of meeting people we think are hot only to have that impression reversed when they open their mouth. The opposite also happens. We meet people and have no immediate chemistry, but after spending a little time with them, we see things about them that we couldn't see right away. Even physical attraction sometimes isn't noticed immediately. Often, even people's looks are not noticeable until they start talking and become animated or smile. Or in his baggy clothes, you didn't pick up that the guy has a great body. Even something so superficial as looks you don't get right away, so of course, you are missing out on the really wonderful stuff by judging men so quickly from your initial "gut" feelings.

Stars are made, not born—and we all have the power to help make people into stars. Many people become better looking when we get to know them. And people tend to blossom when they are happy and nurtured, as they are when they are in good relationships.

When I ask a group of a hundred people in my seminars, "How many of you come across right away, people get who you are quite quickly?" never more than five or six of them raise their hands. Often, I have had groups in which no one raises a hand. Then I ask, "How many of you feel comfortable enough to be yourself on a first date?" Again, no more than six people raise their hands. Then I make the accusation, "Most of you don't come off right away, almost none of you are even present on the first date, yet you have the arrogance to think you have the 'perception' and 'intuition' to be able to read another person so quickly." And you are wrong, just as so many men have been wrong about you because they didn't bother to get to know you.

Women are constantly telling me that they know they can find a relationship. But they don't want just a relationship; they want a soul mate. They want something deep, intimate, and profound. And yet these same women are certain they will be able to identify "the one" by the most superficial means possible.

I am suggesting that you give people more time before you decide to reject them. If you decide at the end of the first date that he is "nice but not my type," I strongly suggest that you employ the Nita Tucker three-date rule: Unless a person is crude, rude, or smells, try to reserve judgment until you have gone on at least three dates. If I hadn't followed this advice (albeit unwittingly), I would not be married today.

I can hear you now, whining that I am telling you to waste your time or to compromise, to be with someone you find physically unattractive. I am not telling you to settle or proposing that you lower your standards. And I am not saying you should have a relationship with someone you find physically repulsive. I think sexual attraction is critically important. I am simply suggesting that you invest a few more hours in getting to know the person better. It is hard to tell right off the bat how attracted you really are to someone. It is not that your expectations are too high; it is just that they are inaccurate.

I ruled out my husband, Tony, as a possible mate when I first met him because I had a very narrow "screening" system based on a strict list of characteristics that added up to what I believed was my type. I dismissed him because I didn't have that gut feeling I got when I was with men I thought were exciting and powerful.

It took me two weeks to get beyond the superficial qualities I found unattractive in Tony. Once I got to know him better, I realized the quietness I had interpreted as weakness was actually more powerful than the kind of forceful machismo I had always equated with strength. I discovered that he had a great sense of humor and that he was sensitive and intelligent. I had been looking so hard for indications of my "type," I had missed most of Tony's best qualities. And the more I got to know him, the more I realized how perfect he was for me.

I was very humbled by this experience. It is easy for me to tell you that you don't know your type, but I was sure I did know my type. I have a master's degree in psychology, and as a consultant, my career depended on my ability to "read" people. I considered myself a much better judge of character than almost anyone, and much more perceptive.

I knew for a fact that Tony was not my type—and I was dead wrong.

I was once a guest on a television show in Seattle. The other guest on the show was the man voted the city's most eligible bachelor. At one point in the show, he looked over at me and commented in a knowing tone, "Nita, you can tell right away if it's going to work out with a woman or not. Isn't that true?" I answered that once I would have agreed with him, but that statement marked the difference between why I was happily married and he was fifty years old and still single.

Ten years of feedback from people who have taken my seminars indicates that the three-date rule made the biggest difference in their dating experiences, and many people claim that if they had not followed it, they would never have connected with their mates.

One of these people is a stunning and very talented woman I know in Los Angeles who complained to me about the lack of romance in her life. "I get asked out all the time," she told me. "That's not the problem. The problem is, I can't seem to find anyone I'm interested in seeing again after the first date. There are just no good men around."

My antennae went up. I recommended that she apply the three-date rule. She went out again, and at the end of the evening, she had the same old feelings of indifference, but she made a second date because she had agreed to try the rule. To her surprise, after the second date, she thought the guy was cute. After the third date, very cute. She told me after about their fifth date that she had never met a more interesting man. I pointed out that she had never given a man that kind of chance before. She, like many of you, was too good at screening people out.

So what if you go out with someone three times and, God forbid, it doesn't turn into a passionate lifetime relationship? I know you would rather spend your precious time reading a book, but spending time with people, finding out what their dreams are, what their lives are like—that is the stuff the books you would rather be reading are made of. Even creeps can be interesting. And even if you still think this would be a waste of your time, you are going to have to waste your time. Because you cannot get who a person is by your first impression. I know you think you can, but it hasn't worked out that way for you. People are far too complex.

All of us operate with a strict set of unwritten rules and guidelines that we use to disqualify people at the encounter stage. I call it the "no" list. The longer your "no" list, the fewer men you will get to know. If you take a good look at your "no" list, you will notice that a lot of your guidelines have nothing to do with what you are looking for in a relationship.

Do you rule out men who are younger or shorter? What about men with beards? Gold chains? Birkenstocks? Maybe you won't date a man who makes less money than you do. You could probably fill a Dumpster with the rules you have about how a person should dress, groom, dance, speak, eat, talk, and walk. You should put these considerations on hold until you get a chance to check out the things that really matter. You know, the stuff that you really end up living with, like the person's convictions and character. A gold chain can be removed; a bad personality is here for the duration.

To decide whether you should continue seeing a man, focus on how you feel about yourself when you are with him. Ask yourself, "Am I having a good time?" "Does he bring out my good qualities?" "Do I feel respected, listened to, attractive?" "Do I like myself when I'm with him?" Ask yourself, "Am I feeling nurtured in this relationship?" Pay very close attention to how you feel about yourself when you are with him. Strong feelings of infatuation can really cloud your judgment. Are you spending most of your time trying to make a good impression? Are you pretending to be someone or something so he will like you better? Try looking at the situation realistically and asking yourself whether there is any true compatibility. I don't care if it is Tom Cruise or Denzel Washington; if you are not having a good time, what are you doing there?

get over it!

The hardest part of having a relationship is what you already know about relationships. It is so difficult to be open, to treat each new person we meet as a new opportunity instead of a reminder of earlier relationships—especially if they were bad. If you cannot be open, the only chance you have is with someone who is totally different from anyone you have ever known, and that isn't going to happen, because before you know it, you will find out that he has something the others had—even if it is just a penis!

Establishing Trust

Because of past failures or hurts, the only lesson many women learned is that they will never let that happen again. They will never give as much as they did, love as much, trust another person with their money, time, love, and life. These women are on the defensive from the start, which is a bigger handicap than being overweight or having crow's-feet.

As I said in Chapter 5, "Clean Up Your Act," nothing is more unattractive than cynicism and bitterness. Women of this type are always there when you want to complain about men and marriage. They know a lot, are full of horror tales, and are ready to compete in a one-upmanship contest with anyone who thinks she got screwed worse than they did.

I have a friend, Laura, who has one of the best stories. She married her college boyfriend, a Harvard man. Rick was everything she was brought up to believe a woman was looking for—tall, handsome, very smart, and from a good family with money. He also had the values that were popular at the time: he was intellectual, sensitive, and deep. By all accounts, he was a great catch. They got married, he started a successful business, they built a fabulous house, and had two beautiful, healthy children. Everything was just as it was supposed to be.

During this whole period, Rick had an interest in spirituality; he read different books on Eastern religion and attended workshops from time to time. After six or seven years of marriage, this interest began to occupy more and more of his time. One day, Laura realized her husband was wearing the clothing required of members of a certain religious sect, which she knew nothing about and was not at all interested in. Over several months, they fought constantly and finally separated. She felt betrayed, shocked, and completely overwhelmed by how misled she had been. "Living with a cult member was definitely not something I had signed on for."

For the next few years, she tried to make her marriage work. She knew she had loved the man, and she certainly wanted to do whatever she could for the children's benefit. She read, attended courses at the ashram, even adjusted her wardrobe. In the end, she couldn't do it; she couldn't live with his "new" values.

Laura is very attractive, extremely intelligent, with a winning and fun personality. So finding another relationship should have been no problem. She definitely was interested in men, except she was more gun-shy than any woman I have ever met. She didn't trust any man to be who he said he was!

I didn't have to delve too deeply to reveal to her that it wasn't men she didn't trust, but herself. This is a smart woman. No one had ever pulled one over on her, and this time she was thrown for a loop. It was as if the rug had been pulled out from under her picture-perfect, secure life.

As long as she thought it was men she couldn't trust, she was terrified to get near another one. It was not until she could forgive herself that she could let another man into her heart and her life. She had to see that it was just a mistake. They were both twenty years old when they met. How could she or anyone have foreseen what he was going to do? At forty-five, she had a much greater sense of who she was and was not nearly as vulnerable to not knowing someone else as well.

The point is that trust resides with you—your trust to see who the other person is, to know whether or not he loves you and is committed to you. As a human being, you are not infallible. You may be fooled. You may make a mistake. That is all the more reason not to rush into something. Let a relationship develop naturally, without the pressure of making it something it is supposed to be instead of letting it be what it is.

Maintaining Your Own Sense of Self

Some of us are afraid of losing our identity in a relationship. It happened when we were younger. Many women went from living at home, where they were totally shaped by the relationships to mother and father—by succumbing to what was wanted and expected or by rebelling against that and refusing to do what was expected; either way, the identity was created and initiated outside themselves—to being in a marriage, and they didn't know any better than to just transfer this responsibility to their husbands and the institution of marriage.

This is what creates the phenomenon of being codependent in a relationship. We only know how to be, by being with someone else. This is what leads to the neediness and desperation that are attributed to many women and are what all of us are so deathly afraid of. This desperation that we feel is very irrational, in that it has nothing to do with independence, financial security, or even a physical taking care of ourselves. It is a much deeper need and attachment that has no rational grounding; we are just very afraid of being alone.

I don't know anything more important to a good relationship than handling this. And the best way to handle this is to be alone for a while. That means not only living alone but not being a couple, not being in a relationship.

For me, this time lasted five years, and it didn't come from self-discipline and abstinence. It came from my not being asked out by anyone. But it was a blessing in disguise because I learned during this time that I could survive without a relationship. When I did get into a relationship, it was because I wanted one. But more important, when I knew I was OK on my own, really knew this, then I became very clear about holding to my standards in choosing a relationship and also in maintaining the standards once in the relationship. My motto became "If it's not going to be exponentially better than living alone, then forget about it."

Now that I am married, I still don't put up with certain behavior or patterns that we fall into; I am not afraid of speaking my mind or risking Tony's anger. I know I will survive even if the marriage falls apart.

I know many women who have experienced the independence that I am talking about, have gone through the time alone, and know it is not awful. They not only survived but have had fulfilling lives. They have a much different fear—that by being in a relationship, they will lose all they have gained.

My friend Cheryl described this experience to me. She

has been successfully on her own for ten years. She is brilliant, beautiful, an accomplished professional with great friends who has traveled the world and has a wonderful home. Recently, she got involved with a great man and is terrified of losing her identity.

She doesn't want him to spend money on her because she thinks that if he does, she will feel obligated or "kept." She worries that she will give up "her voice" in the relationship, that she won't have as much of a say in her own life. She is afraid of moving in together, afraid that she will lose who she is, become a part of him instead of herself, and no longer be the exciting, intelligent, sophisticated person she is. She actually told me she was afraid that, in a relationship, she will become boring. And this is all coming from within; he doesn't have any such expectations of her.

After hearing all this, I told Cheryl I thought she was nuts! She had as much chance of losing her identity and becoming boring as she had of becoming a Martian. In fact, I compared her description of what she feared to the concerns expressed by someone who was afraid of being abducted by aliens.

Even if we *wanted* someone to take away our identity, at this point in our lives, it is not going to happen. You know how hard you have tried to change the men in your life and how you've complained that they have too much baggage for you to be able to make the difference? The same is true about you!

I know the fear is real, but it is totally unfounded. It is based on the past and can really get in the way of your getting what you want in a relationship. As with many other fears, there may be no way to rid yourself of it completely. What I do recommend is that you notice it, recognize it for what it is, understand why you put it there (because you probably had something to be afraid of in your past), and then just step over it and get on with your life.

Exposing Your Attitudes

Many of the bad attitudes you have about relationships came from observing your parents. Even if your parents had a wonderful and inspiring relationship, it may not be useful as a role model for marriage today. That was then, and this is now. But you soaked it up. And not just how they were in their marriage but also every cultural, generational, and personal point of view they held about men and women. And when you grew up and noticed that the world had changed, did you go back and revise these views? No, you didn't even question whether they still applied. You just plopped them down in the middle of your relationship, then wondered why it looked the way it did.

Later, your own relationships became the source of negative attitudes. Whenever you experienced frustration, anger, jealousy, or loss, you racked up dozens of new negative conclusions. If you went through a divorce, you added even more to your already extensive collection of pessimistic beliefs. And along with that lingering sense of disillusionment and failure came decisions like, "I need to take care of me first," or "I'm not going to be taken advantage of again."

You, however, don't live in the restricted world of your parents and grandparents. You don't even live in the world of your last relationship or marriage. You have choices and options. But to the extent that your hidden unquestioned attitudes are dictating your behavior, they are limiting the choices you can make. If your behavior is controlled by negative attitudes and decisions from your past, you are reacting instead of making your own choices. To make choices, you have to release the hold these attitudes have had on you.

Exposing your negative attitudes is the first step toward being able to have the kind of relationship you really want. The next step is to become aware of how these attitudes have been holding you back in your relationships. The third step is to create your own rules, beliefs, and attitudes.

The way your relationships have been turning out has been determined by you, even if that determination has been largely unconscious. Since you are the one in charge, then why not have your relationships be great, powerful, and nurturing? What this takes is to first bring the attitudes and beliefs that are presently running the show to the surface and then sort out the ones you want to keep from those you wish to discard.

Dealing with Divorce

People who are divorced really have to handle what happened in the divorce so that it doesn't overshadow every new possibility of a relationship. Many women are among the walking wounded, suspecting every man they meet to be hiding a land mine beneath his sport coat.

When I ask these women what they are looking for in a relationship, they are very clear—someone *not* like my husband, someone *not* like my previous relationship. This response indicates that they are in just about the worst place they could be.

Most people who want to succeed at something in life look for guidance, information, or support from someone who has already been successful in that pursuit. If you want to make a million dollars today, you are probably more interested in the secrets of Bill Gates than in those of the man who started Wang Laboratories (a once-successful computer company that failed to live up to its initial promise). Young athletes would pay a lot of money to attend a basketball clinic with Michael Jordan.

But somehow I find woman after woman looking to her own and her friends' past failures for information on how to proceed in future relationships. Some of these women have no memory of being loved or getting anything positive out of being married. Others have had horrible divorces.

Instead of learning solely from your mistakes, I suggest you look at what has worked in your past relationships—especially what was great about you in different situations—as your foundation for forming new relationships.

My friend Laurie and her husband were divorced after twenty years of marriage. They had three children, and at one time there had been a great deal of love between them.

Drinking on his part and infidelity on her part had essentially destroyed what they once had. The divorce was terrible! Many years ago, his parents had invested in her business, and now, after more than twenty years of a close family relationship, spending holidays and vacations together, his parents joined their son in suing her. They didn't just sue her; they really tried to destroy her business and livelihood. She felt completely betrayed and devastated that both he and his parents cared more about hurting her than about protecting their children's main source of financial support.

After two nightmarish years of going through this divorce, Laurie, a very attractive and dynamic woman, was certainly interested in dating, but the last thing she ever wanted, *ever*, was to get married again. This has since loosened up a bit, but she still says she doesn't know how she will ever get herself to be truly open again.

Women like Laurie have to work against the defenses they have put up to protect themselves: "I'm never going to let that happen to me. I'm never going to give this much again." The current buzzword for this is *boundaries*, and some of it has to do with finances, but more of it has to do with being open and giving with another human being.

When you start holding back, limiting yourself, and putting up walls between you and another person, you are not available for a relationship—certainly not one that is creative, mature, and better than any relationship you have had before.

Waking Up to Your Patterns

Not everything you learned from your past is bad. For instance, you may have a hidden belief that honesty and integrity are essential to a good relationship. When you bring this to the surface, you also realize that this is a belief you want to maintain as part of your relationship makeup, so you keep it.

The most important point here is that you are always the one designing your relationships, whether you like it or not. Either you can let your unconscious attitudes and beliefs be in charge, or you can choose the ones you want. Once you realize this, the choice is obvious. The only thing required is that you stop complaining about "how relationships are" and be responsible for how you are going to make your relationships.

Sometimes our unconscious attitudes and fears come in the form of "sabotage patterns"—the particular patterns and tendencies we have that damage relationships. I was shocked to discover one of my own patterns one night when Tony and I were having dinner with my girlfriend Leslie only a few months after we had met.

I was proud of my new boyfriend and wanted to show him off. "Tony," I said, "tell Leslie how you got your job with the Sonics." He did, and when he finished, I filled in the parts he had left out.

A few minutes later, I said, "Tony, tell Leslie that funny story you told me last night." Again, he told her, and again, I embellished his story with the details I thought made it more amusing and more to the point. Before long, Leslie and I were doing all the talking. Tony was reduced to playing with objects on the table—his spoon, his water glass, his napkin, my fingers.

By the time we finished dinner, I was embarrassed, angry, and upset. I thought Tony was acting like a jerk. I decided then and there that I would not continue to see him. I couldn't have a relationship with a man who acted like a child.

As we walked across the parking lot to the car, it hit me—a realization so powerful that I will never forget it. Tony had become progressively less interested in talking as the evening wore on. What I saw as childish behavior was his way of reacting to my repeated interruptions and corrections. I guess he figured it was inefficient for both of us to have to say what was on his mind.

Talk about acting like a jerk! I couldn't stand seeing that I had suppressed him in that way. But that wasn't the end of my realization. In a flash, I saw that I had similarly suppressed every man I had ever been with. I hadn't done it on purpose or even consciously; I had done it in such a subtle way that not only had I not seen it, no one else had seen it either. But I saw it now, and the truth was inescapable: I had sabotaged and destroyed every relationship I had had by inhibiting and dominating the men I had gone out with.

I didn't think of it as suppression when I was doing it. I thought I was "helping them improve" or "offering useful advice." In fact, most men I dated told me I was the most perceptive woman they had ever met. But my insights always pointed out their flaws and inadequacies. And after a steady diet of these "insights," they would inevitably lose confidence in themselves.

My explanation for this phenomenon always cast the blame on the man: "He couldn't stand up to a powerful woman," or "He couldn't handle me because I'm too smart." But in that one moment in the parking lot, I saw that I had spent my life looking for a man who would not become dependent, and yet I had always found a way to bring men's weaknesses to the forefront.

For a moment, I hated myself, but then the third part of the realization hit. I saw that my ability to turn men into wimps and bring out their weakness could be turned around. I could use the same power and perception to bring out the best in them. I saw that now I would finally be able to have a successful relationship.

This realization was a major turning point for me. Once I saw how I had been sabotaging my relationships, I could see how to stop doing it.

All the women I have ever worked with have sabotaged their relationships to one degree or another, each in her own way. Often, these women cannot see it themselves— that is, until they look for it. In every case, discovering how they did it has been the first step toward turning it around. And in the course of doing this, they discovered that they— not their mates, their circumstances, or their luck—were responsible for how their relationships turned out.

The first thing to know is that your damaging attitudes and patterns are hidden. That should be quite obvious. If you knew what you were doing to hurt your relationships, you would stop doing it. And not only are your attitudes hidden, but they are also cleverly disguised as "what men always do" or "what keeps going wrong" or "what always happens in relationships." In other words, it is not your fault.

Four Things to Ask Yourself

Question 1: Do I Sabotage My Relationships?

Do you have any sort of recurring problem, large or small, that keeps cropping up in your relationships? If you do (and I have never met anyone who doesn't), you should assume you are the one responsible for it.

The reason you should assume this is not so you can feel bad or guilty about it; it is simply that by taking the position that you are responsible, you can stop this recurring problem from causing damage. This attitude or pattern may never go away completely. You just need to look for it so you can stop yourself before you create a problem, or if you have caused a problem, you can make corrections immediately.

Seeing yourself as the innocent victim is much easier than seeing yourself as the one pulling the strings. But seeing yourself as a victim is never going to make the problem go away. It may sound like bad news that you are the one causing the argument or undermining the relationship, but it is really good news. If you are the one causing the problem, you are the one who can fix it.

Accepting that you are responsible for the problems that surface in your relationships is the most difficult aspect of this process. That is because when you see what you have been doing, you feel like a jerk. It is your natural instinct to avoid being wrong at all costs, so you will probably encounter some resistance to pointing the finger at yourself.

The moment of truth when I saw how I had destroyed relationships with men was awful. Realizing that I had suppressed men did not make me feel proud of myself, but it was the key to my being able to start behaving differently in relationships.

You have two choices. You can consider yourself the victim in your relationships and continue to have the same problems you have had, or you can view your pattern as an inside job and learn how to stop repeating it.

Question 2: Why Do I Sabotage Relationships?

We have already seen that one reason you create problems in your relationships is because of the negative attitudes and fears you inherited from your past. Undoubtedly, there are many other reasons at the root of why people undermine their relationships, but fortunately, it isn't necessary for you to analyze these reasons in order to stop letting them govern your behavior.

In most cases, trying to figure out "why" is just a way of avoiding coming to terms with your pattern and only leads to what is called "analysis paralysis." It wasn't necessary for me to understand all the deep, psychological reasons behind my pattern or to figure out specifically why I suppressed men, nor has it been necessary for any of the couples I have worked with to analyze the reasons behind their patterns.

Telling the truth is what sets you free. Who cares why you have been screwing it up, as long as you stop?

Question 3: How Do I Sabotage My Relationships?

Your modus operandi is a key question. Finding out how you create problems will allow you to stop. In the next section, I describe some of the most popular methods of sabotage, and you may recognize your own among them.

If you don't find your pattern among these few examples, use them as a tool to identify your own. Look not only in your current relationship but in your past ones as well. (Our patterns tend to follow us wherever we go.)

Question 4: How Do I Stop Sabotaging My Relationships?

Once you admit that you sabotage your relationships and discover how you do it, you are ready to reform. The path to rehabilitation is also described in the next section.

Popular Methods of Sabotage

I identify five attitudes or patterns. One or more of them may apply to your situation. Each pattern is broken down into three parts: how you see it, what is really going on, and what to do about it. See if you recognize yourself in any of them.

Attitude/Pattern 1

- *How you see it:* I feel smothered.

Are you most attracted when a man seems aloof or distant? Do you lose interest when he is affectionate or acts adoring? Are you easily bored? Do you get turned off when he gets mushy? Women with this pattern are often uncomfortable with open expressions of love and affection. They prefer that attention and affection be "hard to get" and difficult to come by.

- *What is really going on*

Contrary to what most people who have this pattern think, it has nothing to do with liking a challenge. Instead, it is indicative of a case of low self-esteem—yours. As Groucho Marx once said, "I wouldn't want to belong to any club that would accept me as a member." If you have this pattern, you don't want to be in a relationship with anyone who has poor enough taste to be in love with someone like you.

But if you can't love someone who loves you, you won't be able to have much of a relationship.

- *What to do about it*

Next time a man starts being appreciative and attentive, don't flee screaming and don't pronounce him a bore.

Instead, see if you can bring yourself to endure and learn to tolerate this experience. Give yourself a chance to see how it feels to be liked. Notice how much you want to run away, but instead of doing it, remind yourself that liking you is a sign of someone's good taste!

Attitude/Pattern 2

- *How you see it:* I give more than I get.

Are you always the one who "gives" in your relationships? Do you feel as if you are always there with patience, understanding, and kindness when it is needed, but you never get this treatment in return?

- *What is really going on*

Doormats say "Welcome" on them, and every martyr has to have a persecutor. If this is your pattern, you are not happy unless you are treated less well than you treat others, so you manipulate others into doing just that.

To keep your partner from being as good as you are, you ask him to do things for you when you know he has no time. Or you ask in such an accusatory way that he has to say no. When he does try to do things for you, you don't react graciously; you complain that whatever he did wasn't done right.

True giving is free and is done for the giver's pleasure. If you are keeping score, you are not giving.

- *What to do about it*

It is important for you to keep a close watch on your actions in order to resist your tendency to "give" as a means of manipulating. When you do give, don't keep score. Stop looking at what he or she is doing or not doing for you. When someone *does* do something nice, even something small, be appreciative.

Attitude/Pattern 3

- *How you see it:* My partner says we have a problem, and I don't see it.

Are you always surprised when your partner is unhappy? When a problem is brought up, you may say, "Oh, honey, that's really nothing. I'm sure it will blow over. Don't worry so much." After all, you are sure that *you* would never do anything that annoys—*you* never nag or expect too much. And you are always careful to avoid conflict.

- *What is really going on*

People with this pattern have their heads buried in the sand. By avoiding conflict, you don't have to address any problems that exist in the relationship. You think that if you ignore them, they will go away, but of course, they don't.

When you are unwilling to communicate about anything uncomfortable, there is little to talk about. So much is avoided, there is nothing left to share. A "don't rock the boat" attitude makes relationships boring and mundane.

- *What to do about it*

Start noticing when you want to ignore the issues that arise in your relationship. Stop letting them go by. When your discomfort threatens to keep you from communicating, remind yourself what refusing to confront issues will cost you. When your partner says there is a problem, take it seriously. Stop whatever you are doing and give the matter your immediate attention. Your efforts to trivialize it will only makes things worse.

Attitude/Pattern 4

- *How you see it:* Your partner is threatened by your power.

Does your partner think your opinions are better than his own? Do you feel your strength is overpowering? Are you supportive? Always offering helpful advice? Do you tend to become an "adviser" to the point that he can't do anything without your input?

- *What is really going on*

This was my pattern. I tried to "help" men by pointing out how they could improve and by constantly correcting them. If you have this pattern, you probably consider yourself to be very perceptive. You think you are using your insight to help, but what you are actually doing is constantly finding and pointing out your partner's faults. The message he is getting from you, however subtle, is that he is not OK.

Your partner probably did fine without you. However, once you became a devoted couple, he became dependent. He stopped making decisions, because he knows you will only reverse them. He may have become addicted to your advice. And as he has lost self-confidence, he has become less and less attractive to you.

• *What to do about it*

Start using your intelligence and perceptiveness to build your partner up instead of dragging him down. For example, if he asks you, "What do you think?" instead of giving your usual brilliant answer, ask him what he thinks. Then when he tells you, just shut up and listen. At first, you may have trouble trusting his ideas and responses, because you are so used to your way being the best way. Don't be surprised, though, if the solutions he comes up with are better than yours. Learn to trust his decisions. After all, it was his competence and self-assurance that attracted you to him in the first place.

Attitude/Pattern 5

• *How you see it:* You become a wimp in the relationship.

Do all the ease and confidence you feel in your profes- sional life fly out the window the minute you are in a relationship? Do you avoid saying what is on your mind because you are worried you will look pushy? Do you feel needy and clingy? Do you become intensely focused on the relationship? Do you feel insecure every time you are apart?

• *What is really going on*

You are dependent on your partner for your identity. You are "nobody till somebody loves you." You can probably point to your long list of accomplishments and professional successes to prove how independent you are, but underneath, you feel that you need your partner's approval just to feel all right.

If you are like most people who have this pattern, you seem anything but dependent. In fact, it is your fear of dependency that motivates you to put so much energy into your career. Your achievements are a way of compensating for the desperation you feel about your relationship.

• *What to do about it*

You are so used to covering up your feelings of desperation about needing someone that just admitting you are this way is a great step forward. Next time you notice the desperate or "clingy" feelings coming over you, see if you can just observe them instead of trying to cover them up.

Don't stop achieving, but do stop looking to your accomplishments to provide you with a sense of identity and worth. Your partner loves you for who you are, not for what you have done.

Now What?

You may have clearly recognized your attitude or pattern among those described. You may even have seen yourself in several of them. You may have some but not all of the symptoms of a particular pattern. You may have found a pattern that has shown up in some but not all of your previous relationships. Or you may not have found your particular pattern.

Remember, these are common patterns, and common patterns are never exactly like real life. If the description of a pattern doesn't fit you like a glove, don't quibble. If it has any elements that apply to your situation, you will benefit from taking the position that it is a form of relationship sabotage you are practicing. If you can't identify your pattern, then use the examples as models for how to look for your own. Trust me, there is an unlimited number of patterns out there, and some of them are yours.

Maybe you don't see your pattern clearly or understand yet how you are actually sabotaging your relationships. In that case, assuming responsibility will require a leap of faith. But once you are willing to see yourself as responsible, the insights will dawn on you. There is one thing you can't miss: the common link in every pattern is going to be you.

What if you think you have no pattern? What if you are positive the problem is the men you have been in relationships with but definitely not you? This may seem like a laudable position to be in, but it is not. Unless you can discover the ways you undermine relationships, you will not be able to stop doing it. If the problems in your relationships are not caused by you, you cannot correct them.

What if you see yourself in every pattern? Don't get nervous; you are not a hopeless case, just a bit overanalytical. Focus on reforming the pattern that gives you the most trouble.

Once you identify your pattern, you can begin to turn it around. But don't expect to see it disappear overnight. This behavior is a habit by now, so you will have to exercise discipline in order to stop repeating it.

Before I identified my pattern, I was unaware of my suppressive behavior toward men. Once I knew what to look for, I began to catch myself. At first, just as in the parking lot, I noticed it *after* I did it. With a little more practice, I began to catch myself *while* I was doing it. Eventually, I was able to catch myself *before* I started to behave this way and stop myself. It took discipline just to stick with it at first, but soon the habit diminished in strength.

Remember this: when something is going wrong in your relationship, the trick is to look for *your* pattern. This goes counter to our natural tendency, which is to assume that we are not the ones at fault. But if you are even willing to consider being the one responsible for the difficulty or disagreement, it will give you power—the power to do something about it. In the heat of the moment, it may seem hard to stand back and take responsibility—but believe me, it is less difficult than trying to change your mate.

An added benefit is that when you are willing to take responsibility, it is easier for your partner to do the same and therefore more likely that he will do so. When someone is not being attacked and having to defend himself, it is much easier for him to own up to whatever he may have done to contribute to the problem.

This chapter could backfire if you used this information to analyze your partner's patterns rather than your own. Don't go there! Any efforts you make in this direction will be fruitless. The power to enhance and nurture your relationships will only come from self-awareness.

save sex: the eight-date rule

As I said at the beginning of this book, the one quality that never fails to turn men on is being with a woman who is comfortable with and enjoys her sexuality, a woman who is turned on by and derives real pleasure out of her physical relationship with a man. An authentic enjoyment of your own sexuality and sex is one of the secrets to attracting and holding a man's interest.

That said, however, I am not advising you to jump into bed with the men you date. In fact, when you are dating—whether you are twenty-five or forty-five or even sixty-five—don't have sex too soon. This advice is not based on religious, moral, or health concerns, which are not my fields of expertise, but on my success in counseling people in establishing long-term relationships.

Having sex too soon has kept more potentially good relationships from getting off the ground than any other factor. So even if you are just looking for casual sex, don't have it with someone you may want a long-term relationship with, because you are likely to kill the chances of having that relationship.

The primary reason that having sex too soon interferes with a new relationship is because of what I call the "intimacy gap." This is the gap between the level of emotional intimacy and physical intimacy you experience with someone you just met. The intimacy gap is characterized by confusion ("Where do I stand?") and expectation ("When will I see him again?"). It is the reason for the "morning-after" syndrome, the embarrassment and awkwardness so often felt when you wake up next to someone who is practically a stranger.

When you have sex, whatever your age, it sets up an expectation (or at least raises the question) that this is a relationship. Having this expectation when you have known someone for only a short time is inappropriate. It puts pressure on both of you. At this stage, the bond between you is simply too fragile to withstand this pressure. Instead, it stifles the growth and development that would naturally occur. The result is often that the relationship gets nipped in the bud.

Because of this pressure, one of you—usually the man—withdraws. It is not that he doesn't care, is unfeeling, or was using you. He just doesn't know how to deal with the confusion and expectation. Or if sex doesn't cause one of you to bolt, it can propel you into becoming a couple too soon. This can later result in "buyer's remorse" when one of you realizes that the relationship is not going to work in spite of your initially good chemistry. Initial chemistry is untrust-worthy as an indicator of relationship potential. If there is nothing behind the chemistry, it is better (and easier) to find out before you have sex.

I recommend you wait until you have had at least eight dates before you have sex. The purpose of waiting so long is to support you in taking the time to develop a relationship before you have sex with someone.

Sex Does Not Equal a Relationship

A lot of people have the mistaken idea that if they go out with someone two or three times, it means they are in a relationship. You may be infatuated and feel as if you have known each other forever, but trust me, you haven't. I can-not count the number of times a woman has told me about meeting the perfect man. They had everything in common and talked all night, sharing things with each other they had never told anyone. Inevitably, the end of the story is one night of passionate sex followed by never hearing from him again. If you go too fast or push too hard, no man will stick around long enough for the two of you to determine whether this could be the relationship of a lifetime.

So what do you do when it is your third or fourth date and you really like him? You are excited and turned on. It is late, and he has a long drive home. You do what you tell your kids to do: you wait.

But don't wait until you are locked in his arms to say, "I'd love to make love to you, but I read this book that says we should wait until the eighth date." If this is not your rule, it won't work. You need to think this through and decide ahead of time what you want—not let your emotions in the heat of the moment make the decision for you. Resolving to act in your own best interest ahead of time will leave you better equipped to exercise self-discipline when the time comes. Learn how to say no. "I'd love to make love to you. I just want to wait until we know each other better." Be mature enough to make choices consistent with what you really want.

Remember, the rule is, wait to have sex until the eighth date, not that you have to have sex as soon as you have your eighth date. Many people find that, even on the eighth date, they don't feel they are in a relationship yet. If you have the slightest question in your mind about whether he is going to call or see you afterward, it is too soon. If you aren't sure whether you are ready, err on the side of waiting too long.

By the way, only one date a day counts. If you had break-fast together, then lunch, then cocktails and dinner, then went to a movie, you did not have four dates, you had one long one. (Nice try, though.)

Sex Does Not Equal Love

Many women use sex as a way to feel closer to a man and a shortcut to love. While sex can be an expression of love, it is not a means of achieving love any more than eating in an expensive restaurant is a means of achieving wealth. Having sex because you want closeness, cuddling, and bonding is an approach that usually backfires. Sex can induce these feelings, but they soon wear off, leaving you feeling more lonely and isolated than before.

Intimacy, love, and affection have to be earned. There are no shortcuts. Unless intimacy and love are based on shared experiences, mutual understanding, and appreciation, they have no foundation. They are like a mirage that disappears as you get closer to it. Ask yourself what sex means to you. If it means something, don't do it until that something is there. Don't have sex to try to put it there.

Having sex too soon and creating the expectation that you are now in a relationship often drives a man away. You are also cheating yourself (and the man) out of experiencing the pleasure of sex itself. Although we think men don't care how they get it—as long as they get "it"—we're wrong. They know what's going on and are looking for a woman who really enjoys the sensuousness of sex itself—not someone who is using it to manipulate them. When you are concentrating on where you are going instead of being present to the sensations of "now," you miss out on the only thing that is really available—now.

Casual Sex

At the same time, I do not think you should go too long without sex and affection. In many cases, some casual sex until you find a real relationship is necessary medicine.

My friend Rena was devastated when her husband left

her after twenty-five years of marriage. Fortunately, she had a very successful and demanding career, and she used it to fulfill herself in as many ways as she could. She was able to travel extensively, meet new and interesting people all over the world, and achieve even greater accomplishments in her field.

Three years after her divorce, she was living a life that almost anyone with ambition would envy; she had earned worldwide recognition in her career, and she looked fantastic. The only problem was, she obviously was miserable and had lost the warmth I remembered. Her facade was cold and unapproachable. When I suggested she needed to start dating, she said, "Oh, I'm not ready for a relationship. I haven't gotten over Steve."

"Who's talking about a relationship?" I said. "I'm just talking date—like going to dinner or a movie. What you really need is to be with a man who makes you feel womanly again. I am talking about affection, someone to touch you, and some great sex. Otherwise, I am afraid you are going to shrivel up, dry out, and break. You are missing that glow of someone who has just been freshly f—ked."

She burst out laughing, but it soon turned into tears. She knew I was right. Sometimes you don't need a relationship; you just need sex so you can get your sexiness back, feel attractive, and so looking for a relationship is not clouded by your sexual hang-ups (neediness, insecurity, fears).

I have had women take my seminars who were so serious and uptight about finding a relationship that it was definitely getting in the way. More than once, I have prescribed a trip to Hawaii to have fun and "get laid." Have wild, mad, adventurous sex. Be safe and careful, but let loose, enjoy yourself, and have a great time. This is often the perfect medicine.

Of course, this only works if you give yourself permission to be this way. If you are going against your own morality, it won't work. I want you to feel good about who you are, not hate yourself in the morning. This is also absolutely not an excuse to have an affair with a married man. You will not feel good about yourself if you have any role in an infidelity scenario. I want you to have fun by playing fair with another consenting, unattached adult with no one getting hurt.

To do this, you really have to be honest with yourself. Many times, a woman will respond to a man who says he is only interested in something casual by saying she feels the same way when she really doesn't. She is just agreeing in order not to scare the man away. The truth is, she really is looking for something more serious, especially with this particular man.

Don't lie to yourself and don't lie to anyone else. It won't work and will only backfire on you. You will end up hurt and ashamed.

Unsafe Sex Equals Death

I am continually shocked at how many single people—of every age—don't take the threat of AIDS seriously. These are smart, mature, aware people who are in denial about this very serious issue. They think it is OK to have unprotected sex because somehow the threat of AIDS doesn't apply to them. (In fact, I know one gynecologist who says that, in his experience, the smarter women are, the more likely they are to have unsafe sex!)

I recommend that before you have unprotected sex, you get tested together. Then continue to use a condom for at least six months until you both get tested again. The latest medical evidence says that a waiting period between tests is necessary to establish with certainty that you are not infected. Consult your physician to determine how long you need to wait.

People have told me they don't feel comfortable asking someone to get tested. If you are not intimate enough to be talking about an AIDS test, you are definitely not intimate enough to have sex.

Stop Using Sex and Start Enjoying It

The party line is that men are only interested in one thing—sex. As far as I can tell, that's probably true. Women who clearly don't have the same focus seem to behave as if they did, however—jumping into bed and having sex very early in a relationship.

Most women are not jumping into bed with the first man they see—but instead are jumping into bed with the first man they are interested in, one they regard as having the potential for a relationship.

There is a saying that men use love (romance) to get sex

and women use sex to get love. Neither path seems very honest or satisfying. It is not that the woman wants to make love and have sex; rather, she wants what she will get from the act afterward—the cuddling, closeness, bonding—the feeling that she is attractive and desirable. But what she's really after is to get this relationship on track, to get it to be a "relationship"—her true goal.

getting to "i do"

How to deal with commitment and marriage is the final component of finding and keeping the relationship you want. You may have gotten all kinds of advice about what to do to get a man to make a commitment. Much of this "wisdom" includes how to deal with leftover baggage, setting boundaries, and of course, delivering an ultimatum. In my experience, contrary to helping a relationship, most of these tactics are gimmicks that are at best detrimental and at worst actually destructive to a potentially healthy and enduring relationship.

What I am about to tell you is probably different from what you have heard before. Feedback from the thousands of women who have read and used this advice is that (1) they didn't like hearing it, and (2) this advice has been the missing link for them. Personally, based on my own success and the success of so many others, this is "the real gold."

A great, fun, wonderful, nurturing relationship evolves

quite naturally into commitment. Two people go out, have a good time, and so they want to spend more time together. They spend more time together, that time is good, they get even closer, and so they want to spend more time together. That time is great, so they do more, talk more, get more intimate. If that goes well, they get closer and, of course, want to spend more time together. This happens naturally—no force is required—*if* the relationship is good, fun, and nurturing.

Contrary to popular belief, commitment is not a declaration; it is not there by someone's saying it is there; it is there because it is there. And it is very easy to distinguish whether someone is committed to you or not. How you know someone is committed to you is by a physical "touch test." How you know someone is committed to you is that he is there. Just as how you know someone is rejecting you is that he is not there. If someone is with you, wanting to be with you, standing by your side when you need him, then he is committed. It is simple, right?

No way, not for us women. We start dating a man, and things are great. We are both having fun. We are close, intimate; we keep wanting to be together. We make the time for each other, and everything's hunky-dory. Then what do we do?

"We need to talk about our relationship. Where do you see the relationship going? Are you serious? If you aren't serious, when are you going to get serious? What do you need to know or do or handle in order to get serious? Are you going to make a commitment? If so, when? If not, what do you need to do to make a commitment? What's wrong with me? What's wrong with you? You must have some baggage from past relationships you need to handle. We need to work on this. I'm not going to be with someone who's not going to make a commitment. I'm not interested in just having fun and being loved; I need to know where this is going and when. You're probably commitmentphobic and should see someone about it. That's it." And finally, the last threat: "I'm setting an ultimatum. If you don't make a commitment by __ [date], we're through!"

When I grew up, commitment meant that men in white coats came and took you away. I think many women are doing their fair share to keep this interpretation intact. Women want men to make a commitment, to say it, write it in blood, and put money down on the deal. So women take a man who is committed (proved through physical evidence of the man's being there) and tell him he now needs to make a commitment—which is, in essence, saying that the man is not committed. Right?

A woman takes a man who is already committed and tells him he is not committed again and again until she is right. Women take men who are committed and they invalidate and squash the commitment out of them. Women are commitment killers! Nurturers of relationships? Are you kidding me? They are murderers! Like crusaders, in the name of love and relationship, they are leaving in their wake the wreckage of the relationships they have trampled and destroyed.

Are You Your Own Worst Enemy?

When I interview women about what an ideal relationship would look like in their lives right now, they say they really want someone who loves and adores them. They like the life they have, but they want someone to talk to every day, to share their life with, someone who cares about what is happening, cares about what the women are going through in their lives, not necessarily involved in everything they do but interested and supportive.

Also, almost every woman says she wants a man who has his own life and does not depend on her to fulfill all his needs, such as feeling useful, productive, and entertained. So although "partner" is the cliché that is often used in describing the ideal mate, I have found that most women are looking instead for a great friend and an attentive, passionate, and caring lover.

This is what I mean when I say we women need to get clear on what we really want in a relationship, not what we are programmed to want, nor what we wanted when we were twenty or thirty. We need to look at the life we're living now, our present needs and desires, and adjust accordingly.

"Well, I'm not looking for a casual relationship. I can't give my love without it meaning something, without it being serious, without a commitment." I agree with this point of view and think it is quite mature. But you can't make someone committed to you if he is not, and you don't find out whether someone is committed by having him prove it and "make a commitment."

Those of you who are divorced know that vows do not a commitment make. You have to let the commitment develop naturally; you have to be patient and give it time. "But I don't want to waste my time on a relationship that isn't going somewhere." My answer to this is, if you are having fun, if you feel great about yourself when you are with this man, if you are feeling love and loved, then how could you be wasting any time? And if you don't feel this way with the man, then you know for sure that this is not someone with whom you want a commitment!

Avoiding Failure

In our culture, manhood is measured by success. Typically, men are brought up with the notion that, to be a man, you have to prove yourself and be successful. For most men, there is nothing worse than failing. (Women don't like failure either, but it is not as central to their sense of identity. Being considered ugly is the female counterpart.) And even if a man does fail, there is a silent conspiracy not to mention it. That is why we have euphemisms such as "downsizing" and "transitioning" to mask a man's failure in the workplace.

A huge percentage of single men over thirty are divorced. If they aren't divorced, their parents or their best friends or their next-door neighbors or both their sisters are. The divorce rate now is more than 55 percent; it is an epidemic. *Newsweek* called it a plague. So divorce is looming over all single men even if they haven't gone through it themselves.

I don't care what the circumstances were; a divorce is a failure. People don't go down the aisle and say, "If everything goes as planned, in about ten years, we should be filing for separation." No matter how much a man might justify a divorce—"I'm much happier now," "It was best for the kids," "We parted on good terms," "We still like each other; we just weren't right for each other"—deep down, it is still registered as a failure.

When a man has a failed relationship or two under his belt, he begins to get wary. As a result, he may be gun-shy about committed relationships and not have a clue that this is really about a fear of repeating failure. On a conscious level, he may want a relationship and even ardently pursue one. When he talks about the family life he values, he means it. But when things develop to the point at which a commitment is in the offing, something happens. As soon as it looks as if "This is it," he freaks out and doesn't know why.

What is happening is that he is reminded of the last time things got this close. Warning bells go off. "I can't have a failure," he thinks. "I certainly cannot be a two-time [or three-time] loser." The problem is, this thought process is unconscious. The result is a man who goes like gangbusters toward a relationship, then suddenly withdraws.

I get phone call after phone call from women who tell me, "He was the one who pursued the relationship. He was the one who wanted to get serious. He was the one who wanted to move in. And now he's backing out."

I experienced this phenomenon myself when I was dating Tony. After we had been going together for several months, he asked me to move in with him. I wasn't so sure I wanted to. I didn't care for his suburban Seattle neighborhood, preferring my place in the city. But I went along with the move because of his insistence, and because I loved him.

My first clue that things weren't going well was that when I was unpacking, Tony, who is normally very helpful, was nowhere to be seen. When I looked for him, I found him sitting alone in the dark. I asked him what was going on. He gave me the classic male answer: "Nothing."

Suddenly, I sensed what was happening. I asked him if he was feeling trapped. "Yes," he replied, as if in a trance. My first reaction was to kill him. This wasn't even my idea. I wasn't even moving into a place I liked—and he was accusing me of trapping him! Justification for homicide.

Fortunately, it dawned on me that the divorce he had been through shortly before I met him was behind all this. I thought, now he is setting up housekeeping again; it must be pretty scary. We started talking about what he was going through. I suggested that maybe it was too soon for us to be doing this and offered to move back to my apartment. He said, "No, I want you to be here. This was my idea."

We went out for dinner and had a very romantic evening. Things went great for about a week. Then one night we were sitting in the living room, talking. I mentioned the idea of our taking a vacation together that summer. All of a sudden, I noticed his eyes begin to glaze over. He looked upset and became withdrawn. I could practically see the word *trapped* appear across his face. It was obvious to me but invisible to him.

During the next few months, whenever we talked about the future—planning a vacation, holidays, anything that made this seem like a permanent relationship—I would see the same signs. Each time I noticed the signs, I would ask, "Are you feeling trapped right now?" He would say, "Yes, I am," and I would say, "Oh."

Each time the signs surfaced, I tried to help Tony understand what he was going through. I had to keep reminding myself to be compassionate, to try to look at what was going on from his point of view. I had to remember each time not to take it personally and not to be hurt by it. This was his process, not mine. I didn't ignore his fear, but neither did I get angry or defensive or try to change the way he felt. I just understood what he was going through and that he was entitled to these feelings. After four or five months, he got through it.

Dealing with Men's Withdrawal

All too often, women take it personally when a man begins to withdraw. When he starts pulling back, her interpretation is that he doesn't love her as much as he used to. She gets hurt. This only exacerbates the situation, because most men, like most women, hate hurting another person. The woman's hurt feelings can cause the man to pull even further away because of the guilt he feels in response.

This generates a vicious cycle. Often, the outcome is that the man leaves—not because he doesn't care about the woman but because he does. He is trying to escape from the pressure and guilt he feels over hurting someone he cares about.

It is important to know how to handle this phenomenon when it rears its ugly head, because the truth is, this happens more often than not.

The first step—assuming you have not already destroyed the relationship with your goals, demands, and invalidation of the already existing commitment—is to acknowledge that the man is pulling back. He is already in denial that this is happening, so if you ignore it, too, it will not go away but only get worse.

The next step is to be compassionate about what he is going through. Compassion is seeing it from his point of view. Many women complain that they have been patient and compassionate, but now they have to take care of themselves. But I say your whining and demands are the opposite of compassion.

Far from being compassionate, many women are angered and disgusted by men exhibiting this behavior. I must admit that I, too, once felt this way, but now that I have looked into this from every angle, including my own, I see it much differently.

I am certain this behavior of pulling back comes from

men's integrity. It has next to nothing to do with a fear of commitment. A man does not want to give his word unless he is sure he will be able to keep it. If you look at the shape of the institution of marriage nowadays, the chances are high that this marriage, too, won't last. Most definitely, a man does not want to give his word again if he has already failed.

Far from seeing him as emotionally weak or impaired, I now find it sexy that a man wants to succeed and hates to fail. I find it even more attractive that a man's word and integrity are so important to him.

You can begin to imagine what a difference it would make if women started regarding a man's hesitancy from this point of view. It would obviously be much more productive for both parties.

The second step is not to take it personally when a man pulls this number. Admittedly, it is difficult not to be hurt when the man you love starts to withdraw, but trust me, you have got to stay out of his process. This is not about you. (I know, *everything* is about you.) Here we have a man who is freaked out, doesn't know why he is freaked out, but somehow does recognize that whatever is freaking him out is hurting you. He has no choice but to leave.

What women tend to do at this point is ask the man, "What's wrong with me? What don't you like about me? What about me are you unsure of, or what do I need to change in order for you to be sure?" Can you see the pattern here? Can you see who is the subject of this interrogation?

All you can get from this line of questioning are answers that have nothing to do with the cause of the situation, answers you don't really want to hear.

Before you opened your mouth, the man was at a loss about why he was hesitant. Now you, in your infinite wisdom, have given him the reasons why he must be so unsure. You have told him it has to do with you and your inadequacies, and now you have him convinced. I am sure you can see why this approach is not working.

I tell women, if you can't help but take this personally and make it be about you, wave at the same time, because he will not stay around and hurt you. If you must get hurt, hit your head against the wall; just don't beat yourself up by putting yourself in the way of his process.

The last step is to come to the table with confidence in yourself (once again, this quality surfaces) and in the relationship. The truth is, you know that he loves you, and you probably even know (from the touch test) that this man is committed to you. Why would you seek a commitment with a man unless you were sure of his love?

In order to be successful in having a committed relationship, you have to stop playing this game of "If you love me, you would __ [commit to me, marry me, buy me a diamond ring]." Either he loves you or he doesn't, and you know which it is. How demeaning to both of you to need proof!

Instead, when a man starts to back away, respond by saying, "It's getting scary isn't it? But we have something great, and you're going to have to risk it. Besides, the truth is, you're already committed. And I know we can make this relationship work. The water is fine; you can come in."

Many women come to my seminars hoping to find out how they can screen out these "emotionally handicapped" men. They say, "I want to be able to tell right away if a guy is commitmentphobic or emotionally unavailable. I don't know how many more times I can handle falling in love and having my heart broken. Please tell me how to identify these men from the start."

But labeling "these" men is too cheap and too easy. You want to know how to pick them out? That is easy—men, pretty much all of them. It is predictable that men are going to go like gangbusters into a relationship and then pull back when they get into the danger zone of potential relationship failure. Be prepared.

Do you know why men are hesitant to make a commitment? They want assurance that this is a "bombproof, failureproof, divorceproof" relationship. All these great risk takers want no part of the risks in this situation. Their threshold for rejection and failure was reached by the time they were eighteen, and they can't tolerate any more. This is why men aren't asking women out on dates. They don't even want to go out for coffee without this guarantee that the woman is the "one" forever and ever.

Neither you nor anyone else can give a guy the guarantee he wants. But just as your lack of confidence is enough to drive him away, your display of confidence and support are usually enough to give him the confidence he needs.

After I have talked about these commitment patterns in my seminars, I look out at the audience, and you wouldn't believe all the guilty faces I see. I tell the women, "Breathe. You're not an awful woman. We all do this." After the seminar, I can count on at least three women coming up to me to make the confession, "I did that. I was with a man for four years, and I nagged him about making a commitment the whole time until I finally drove him away. I see now that, of course, he was committed. What else was he doing for four years! He just wasn't following 'my program,' and now I've lost him. Is there any hope left at this point?"

My advice is that it is worth a try, one try. It is very hard to rehabilitate a relationship, especially if he won't return your phone calls. But it is worth one try. If you do get in touch, be very, very light. Just say, "Let's get together for dinner or a movie." *Do not say, "Let's get together to talk about the relationship!"* Just get together to have fun and be together, and if it does fall back into place, don't you dare bring up the old conversation, "Are you ready now for a commitment? When will you reach the point of being ready for a commitment? Are you going to start pulling back now?" Don't you dare!

Because he will start pulling back, and you will lose your second (and most likely last) chance to deal with this as a grown-up, mature woman. Knowing these steps and following them make the difference between murdering a relationship and expanding and furthering it. We all know of women who put up with a man for many years who wouldn't commit, and then they break up and he marries someone else four months later. You may think the second woman was benefiting from all the groundwork laid by the first. I disagree. I say the second woman knew how to handle the fear of failure.

You really need to remember this chapter. In fact, I recommend that you keep this book on your nightstand with a bookmark in this chapter because you will forget and get sucked in again and again.

My friend Cynthia called all excited about the new man in her life. "This guy is amazing, Nita, he's totally different. He *wants* a relationship. We've talked about it, and we want the same things. We've even discussed where we want to build a house together!" Well, all kinds of red flags went up for me, but not wanting to burst her bubble, I tactfully mentioned that she should be prepared for him to start pulling back in around three to six weeks. "Oh, no, Nita, not this one. He's different. He's clear about what he wants and where he wants this relationship to go."

I hate to sound smug, but of course, I was right. At week four, Paul did the predictable. Cynthia was naturally dismayed at first, but fortunately, she was prepared, handled it beautifully, and now they are engaged and planning the wedding.

You can't undo your past mistakes, but you sure can learn from them. If you haven't experienced this particular relationship "ballet" before, then be smart and learn from the mistakes of others.

How Men Can Benefit from This Information

I tell men they should try to be conscious about what they are going through and to understand that it is about fear of failure, not fear of commitment. Men have now been told by so many women that they are afraid to commit, they have started to believe it. I can't tell you how many men have described themselves to me as "a man who can't commit." They are reading books about their "commitment-phobia" and going on weekend drumming workshops in the woods with their men's groups to try to get over it. There is nothing wrong with that; it is just that they are treating the wrong disease.

What About Marriage?

The biggest adjustment that needs to be made regarding finding a relationship when you are after forty is in what you are looking for. We are so different at forty than at twenty: our lives are different; our interests are different. Hopefully, we are more mature, evolved, and our needs are different. Yet it seems little has changed. Most women want to get married.

When you are forty or fifty, there probably are not a lot of reasons to get married. I am not saying that you shouldn't get married or that marriage has no purpose at this age, but there is very little need to get married, nor is there much logic in doing so. In fact, logically, there are probably more reasons not to get married. Finances are much more complicated as you get older, especially if there are children involved. You probably are not interested in starting a family, so there is no need to get married to provide a foundation for a family. Individual careers and established homes and lifestyles can be difficult to blend, which dating someone does not require but marriage does.

Yet the name of the game in relationships, the goal or finish line, always seems to be commitment and marriage. We are driven by this "end," and I suggest that it is not what we really want. Worse, this drive is sabotaging our real needs and wants. Even if what you want is marriage, focusing on it is the cause of the majority of failures in this area. Women keep trying to get somewhere—married. In the meantime, they neglect the present, which is the only place a relationship exists.

We women cannot stand to live with the discomfort of loving and being loved *and* the possibility of losing that love. Out of fear, we feel compelled to trap our feelings rather than risk their getting away. We don't trust the man, but even more tellingly, we don't trust ourselves to allow these feelings to grow and blossom. And we are right not to trust ourselves, because the moment these feelings appear, we rush to capture and preserve them in the nearest available airtight Tupperware container.

As much as we claim to hate institutions and fear acting in an automatic, institutionalized, and rigid way, that is just what we are doing. It is our own automatic, driven, obsessed behavior that must be exposed and tried before a jury of our real needs and desires to see if this behavior is really serving us or if we are serving it.

The first place to look is the question "Why get married?" The original purpose for marriage was the survival of the species. Men provided food and shelter, while women had babies and cared for them. This reasoning, and the roles that came with it, hasn't evolved much until very recently. At its best, marriage provides a secure, stable environment for the raising of children in the form of emotional, social, economic, intellectual, and spiritual guidance and nurturing.

One highly educated, newly divorced woman suggested that I use this book to devise an alternative to marriage for women with grown children. She sees a need for a viable, positive alternative to marriage that is durable and is socially and morally accepted. (Cohabitation is very common today but is still looked on with a tinge of disapproval.)

While I see her point, I think a more realistic approach is the creation of a self-determined purpose and structure for a relationship, custom-designed by each couple rather than dictated by accepted, outdated customs and history.

My friend Lauren got married at age forty-three. She already had children, an established career, a fulfilling and nurturing community of friends and family, and was financially independent. She has a wonderful husband and loves being married. While discussing the outdatedness of marriage, I asked her if she would still get married.

She answered, "Absolutely," and was quite certain of her reasons for choosing marriage over an undeclared (or even declared) commitment. Her primary reason for marriage was to establish "family" with the man she loved. This is a woman who had no shortage of close familial bonds but who felt strongly about extending these relationships to include her husband and his family. She reminded me that an immediate family unit did not have to include children to experience family.

She went on to quote my previous book, *How Not to Screw It Up*, in which I say that how you talk about your relationship is how it is, or at least has a dramatic influence on how it is, for you. In marriage, she said, you not only declare your relationship publicly through your vows; you are actually acting upon them through the act of getting married.

She also quoted me on the importance of having a community to support your marriage. "Sure, marriage is an institution, but that's a positive thing, too." Even though divorce is very common, the institution of marriage gives you much more of a structure to work within than cohabitation. When you are having a fight or difficult times, it is a lot harder to walk away when you are married. The boundaries aid you in sticking with it, getting through it, and in most cases building an even stronger bond.

Marriage is something to be looked at very carefully and for the right reasons. If you find yourself driven to get to the finish line called wedding, you really have to stop and examine why and for what. I constantly tell women to stop worrying about where they are going and start enjoying where they are. You may soon discover that you are already in exactly the place you were hoping to get to.

OK, but How Do I Get to "I Do"?

My advice is, don't get married until you already are. If love and commitment are not present in your relationship, getting married won't put them there. If they are there, you are already married. Then you can have a ceremony as a celebration of that fact. I personally believe in marriage, because I think "going public" in this way creates a kind of community support. Relationships are tough; you need all the support you can get.

Left to their own devices, many men would not express their commitment by getting married. Therefore, it is often up to women to provide the impetus for taking this step.

A lot of women have told me, "If he loved me, he would marry me." Not necessarily. Marriage is not a man's sport. There is no such thing as *Groom's* magazine. You don't often hear men saying, "My whole life, I've dreamed of standing there watching my future wife come down the aisle. I've always looked forward to renting a tuxedo and choosing a silver pattern."

After I had been living with Tony for about eighteen months, I knew it was time for us to get married. I already knew that we loved each other and were both committed to this relationship. I said, "Tony, I think it's time for us to get married." He said, "I don't really want to." I said, "Fine. I was thinking June or September." He said, "OK, make it September." In the end, because we wanted to have our wedding on a boat in Puget Sound, we got married in July.

This approach worked because it was not about Tony's

proving that he loved me or was committed. I knew he would never volunteer for marriage, but I also knew that this was not a reflection of how he felt about me. It was the generic male resistance to marriage. To pull this off, you must be absolutely certain of the relationship.

My inspiration for this approach was my friend Claire. She was a real master—and it is a good thing she was, because her boyfriend, Martin, had the most severe allergy to marriage of any man I have ever met.

Claire and Martin had been living together for seven years when she told him it was time to get married. He didn't want to. But he didn't want to lose her, so he agreed.

They asked me to meet with them to help them plan their wedding. When I arrived at their apartment at the agreed-upon time, Martin wasn't home yet. Normally a punctual person, he arrived forty-five minutes late.

The three of us sat down with our lists and pages of notes and started to plan the wedding. Martin got up to get something from the kitchen and came back ten minutes later. We resumed the meeting. Five minutes later, he left abruptly to make a phone call. This sort of thing went on for about an hour.

Finally, I asked Martin what was wrong. "Nothing," he said. Claire said, "You don't want to get married, right?" There was a pause, then Martin sighed and said, "No, I don't."

I thought Claire would cry or get mad or be devastated, but she just said, "I understand. What do you want to do about this?"

Martin said he wanted to go out for a walk. After he left, I turned to Claire and asked, "Are you devastated? Does this mean the wedding's off?" She said, "No, it just means he doesn't want to get married. He never wants to go out and run either, but he always does it anyway, and then he's glad he did. This is the same kind of thing."

"Don't you feel bad that he's not enthusiastic about marrying you?" I asked. "Of course," she said. "I would like it better if he were sweeping me off my feet instead of kicking and screaming over this, but I know he loves me and is committed to this relationship. When he talks about not wanting to get married, I don't argue with him. I just keep going forward with our plans, because I know this is a process he needs to go through."

As it turned out, Martin got over his resistance later, not sooner. He had second thoughts until his wedding day. But the wedding proceeded as planned, and they have been happily married for the past twenty years.

In working with hundreds of men, I have met very few who wanted to get married. I have met lots, however, who got married.

Women constantly tell me they don't want to settle. As I have said all along, I agree that you shouldn't settle. Yet I see women settling all the time.

Living alone when you want to share your life with someone, being with friends when what you want is a passionate love in your life, not loving or being loved when your body and soul are aching for it—that is settling. Many women have given up on what they want and are settling for a "second-best" kind of life, a consolation prize.

Don't do this. If there is one thing I have learned at the deepest levels from the most hard-core cases over many years of working with people on finding relationships, it is that *you* can have the relationship you want.

You now know "the secret" and know what tools you need to develop to find not just some man but a fulfilling and passionate love, a relationship that, in the words of the movie character Jerry McGuire, "completes you." All it takes is for you to go out and do it.

living happily ever after

Everyone knows you can't talk to someone in love about the things he or she will need to know when the honeymoon is over. Don't wait until you are in a relationship before you read my book about keeping your relationship nurturing, fulfilling, and passionate—*How Not to Screw It Up*. After all, most of us start screwing up our relationships right away. So let's talk about it while you still have your wits about you.

Excerpts from *How Not to Screw It Up*

Most people don't get married with the idea that there's a pretty good chance their marriage will not last. But in fact, 75 percent of first marriages and 55 percent of marriages overall are ending in divorce—which means more couples are divorcing than staying together. Yet couple after couple walk down the aisle knowing their marriage is different, or this marriage is different from their previous one(s), and therefore, it will last. And what are they doing to ensure that they will not be another statistic of failure? Nothing.

The problem is, we've been taught and conditioned to think there is nothing to do after the "I do." This book is about some things you can do—not only to prevent divorce but to have an extraordinary, healthy, fulfilling relationship.

Dispelling the Modern Myths about Marriage

The three most commonly held ideas about marriage today are:

1. It takes constant work to have a successful relationship.
2. Both parties in the relationship need to be committed to the success of the relationship; in other words, a good marriage is a fifty-fifty proposition.
3. When couples grow apart, it is sufficient and legitimate cause for divorce.

Based on these three ideas, it is quite possible to find yourself feeling anxious and burdened by your relationship rather than nurtured and happy. It doesn't have to be that way. This book is based on two radical ideas that counter the current myths about marriage:

1. It only takes one person to have a healthy, happy relationship.
2. What there is to do is a matter of fun and play, not work.

If you are willing to entertain those two possibilities, then the challenges and problems that come along—even from something as apparently fatal as growing apart—not only can be dealt with successfully but can leave you with an even stronger, closer relationship.

Who Should Read This Book

After taking my couples workshop, one participant's comment was, "This course should be a prerequisite for getting a marriage license." This book is the answer to that need and provides the insurance that newlyweds or new couples are looking for. It is just as relevant, however, for those who want to ensure that their long-term relationships will last and continue to grow and deepen.

Your relationship doesn't have to be in trouble for this book to be useful. If it is in trouble, however, this book could save it. If you are not about to get divorced but your relationship feels old and tired, this book will wake things up and make it feel exciting and passionate again. And even if only one of you reads this book and takes it to heart, that is sufficient to make the difference.

This book is not a substitute for marriage counseling or professional therapy. It is a guide for couples who want to acquire the skills to keep their relationships in top form. If you read it and do the creative exercises at the end of each chapter, you, too, can have results in your relationship that exceed your expectations. You will have the tools to deal with whatever comes along in your relationship as well as the tools to create an extraordinary, passionate, and exiting love beyond your dreams. You, too, can have a relationship that is better than it was when you first met—not just good enough to last but profoundly nurturing and satisfying—and without having to get a new partner.

Stop Focusing on What's Wrong and Start Getting What You Want

Most loving relationships begin with two people in wild appreciation and adoration of each other. But over time, many deteriorate to the point where the couple can only speak about their marriage in terms of what doesn't work.

I've asked couples how their relationships were when they first got together. Instead of telling me how in love they were, they tell me all the things that were wrong: "We were very young. We thought we had to be married to live together. We didn't really know each other. All our friends were getting married, so we did, too." But I don't buy this. I don't believe that these people were so stupid as to marry someone they didn't love. These weren't shotgun weddings. These people got married because they were in love— maybe immature, but still in love.

The first step to a rebirth of the relationship is to remember who and what you fell in love with.

A few years ago, Bob and Sharon, a couple who complained that their relationship not only was not working but was dead, came to my seminar. They weren't ready to leave each other, they said, nor were they having affairs. There just wasn't any life left in their eighteen-year-old marriage. I asked them to tell me what was great, what was the best thing about their relationship. "We don't bother each other. We let each other do whatever we want," they said. Their mutually shared focus on staying out of each other's way was the *best thing* they had to say about their marriage!

I made them dig deeper to tell me what it was like when they were first together. After a few moments of hesitation and struggle, they began to remember how much fun they used to have. Sharon told me about Bob's playfulness and several of his practical jokes. Bob recalled what a buddy she was; she was a great sport, and he could do anything with her. Soon they began to get back in touch with the qualities that had attracted them to each other in the first place. By the end of the seminar, both of them had rediscovered wonderfully stimulating and lovable aspects of the other. So much so that Bob was bragging about how much fun she was, and you could see that the passion had returned to their marriage.

The Order of Things to Come

There is a natural progression or, more accurately, regression in any relationship. You fall in love with someone, and everything about him or her is wonderful, miraculous, enchanting. You love the way he is with his family, the way he listens to you. The way she tilts her head is so graceful, and you love her mischievousness. You are endlessly fascinated and enthralled with every movement, every touch. And you express the thrill of it all. You tell your new love how sensitive and special he is. You tell your parents and your friends that she is the most warm and giving woman you've ever met.

You know how nauseatingly people go on and on when they're first in love? Family and friends put up with it because they know it will pass. Sure enough, it does. And then something happens, or an imperfection peeks through. She's always late, or he watches too much television. In a way, even this stage feels good at first—as if having a problem to work out is a signal that this is a relationship to take seriously. When your friends ask you how things are going, you can say, "Great, but we have a few issues we need to work on."

Everything is as it should be, except for this "one thing." This is where we decide that what it is going to take to make everything perfect again is work. This is also where appreciation begins to take a backseat to our efforts to make everything fit our ideas of how we think it should be. And more often than not, it is the beginning of the end of a great relationship.

You don't have to do anything about the good things because "if it ain't broke, don't fix it," right? So you devote lots of attention to this problem thing. You discuss it with each other, you read books about it, and you seek advice from friends. Meanwhile, less and less of your attention goes to those great qualities you fell head over heels in love with, the reasons you got married in the first place. There seems to be an unspoken agreement that you don't need to pay attention to "how generous she is" or "how sensitive he is." Those qualities are fine; they don't need any correction or improvement.

Eventually, we are only paying attention to the problems. And since problems get the focus, problems are all we see and experience. The nonproblematic things that we used to dote on, the things that enamored us so, fade far into the background from lack of attention.

This is how we take a fulfilling, nurturing, exciting relationship and kill it. Almost everyone does it, too. Here's proof: how many lively and passionate longtime relationships do *you* know of?

Use It or Lose It

What is not appreciated does not last. We all know the story about the attractive woman who gets married and then lets her looks go. The usual line of gossip is that she only took care of herself to get married. I find this isn't usually the case.

The good-looking woman who keeps herself fit and well groomed discovers early in her relationship that her boyfriend or fiancé likes this about her. He compliments her looks, her new hairstyle, or how great that dress looks on her. She blossoms from his attention. His expressions of admiration make her feel attractive and loved, and she makes sure she continues to look great because he notices.

After a period of time, however, probably well after the wedding, he starts taking her beauty for granted and stops paying attention to how she looks. He is happy to see her at the end of the day but rarely compliments her on her appearance. One day, she comes home with a new hair color, and he doesn't even comment. Soon after, she begins to think it's no big deal if she wears the sweat suit she's been wearing all day or if she doesn't wash her hair as often. He doesn't notice anyway. Next, she starts skipping her workout—also no big deal.

She doesn't put much effort into how she looks anymore, because it doesn't seem to matter. And because her attractiveness is no longer acknowledged, there is no longer any of the original pleasure or reward for her.

Nothing is mentioned about her appearance again until the day he notices the emergence of some new growth in her hips. *Then* he speaks up and tells her she's "got some new fenders on the chassis." So now, because once upon a time he expressed his admiration for her looks in glowing compliments and attentive remarks but has said nothing for a long time and has just criticized her with a wisecrack, there is a "problem." *He* has lost the beauty he cherished, and *she* has lost her appreciative and sensitive man (not to mention those slim hips).

It is a red flag signaling trouble when something that was once wonderful in a relationship begins to disappear. This is your wake-up call that you have been taking your spouse for granted. Immediate attention is required.

Sometime back, I appeared on a morning talk show in Houston while on tour promoting my last book. After the show, the producer came up to introduce himself and thank me. This man was one of the most sexy, magnificent-looking men I had ever laid eyes on. So when he asked if he could attend the seminar I had scheduled for that night, I said yes, of course. *(Are you kidding!)* As it turned out, he later left a message saying that he wouldn't be able to make the seminar but would like to meet me afterward and take me to dinner.

When I got home the next day, my husband, Tony, asked me about the trip, and I told him I went to dinner with the TV producer and almost got in trouble.

"And how did the show go?" Tony asked, to which I replied, "Tony! Wrong question! I just told you I had dinner with a man and almost got in trouble."

I travel alone all over the world. I work with and see lots of men. Almost never do they come on to me. It's not that I'm unattractive. It's just that I don't put out the vibes that invite advances. I did, however, in Houston.

Tony finally got the point. And so did I. I was looking around because he had not gotten his job done, the job of paying me the kind of attention that makes me feel attractive and desirable. I needed to feel I was attractive and sexy, and Tony was the one I really wanted to make me feel that way. Furthermore, if Tony forgot to do his job, then it was up to me to ask him directly to do it—not try to remind him by flirting or worse.

This is a good example of the kind of "problem" we could have worked on. Instead, we saw that we simply had been neglecting our expressions of affection and appreciation for each other. Restoring those qualities to our relationship was not something either of us considered work; it was quick, easy, and fun.

If It Ain't Broke . . . Love it!

If it worked to focus on what doesn't work in a relationship, I would support it as a method for dealing with the issues that inevitably arise in relationships. But it simply doesn't work! It doesn't solve problems or make things better.

I know couples who have been together forty years, and the same complaints between them are still rampant: he's always late and doesn't communicate, and she still spends too much money. Years of critical attention and focus haven't changed the problems at all, except perhaps to have made them bigger. Problems have become the core of these relationships, and any delight with each other has long since wasted away.

Patterns or habits of taking each other for granted can set in early in the relationship. Tony and I had been together about a year when he came home from work one evening, kissed me, and sat down with the newspaper. I sat next to him and watched him read. After a few minutes, I took the paper and put it aside. Then I took his hand and walked him out the front door.

"We are going to do this again," I said. "I refuse to spend evening after evening *watching* you read the paper. You happen to be very lucky to live with me, and if you don't treat this relationship as special and express how fortunate you are, you don't get to keep it. Now, walk in again and show me that you're thrilled to see me, that you feel lucky to be with me. And show me all this without looking as if I'm an obstacle on your way to the newspaper."

Tony told me he realized from this interaction what had happened in his first marriage. To the observer, Tony had been the nice guy in the marriage, his wife was the shrew, and he was smart to leave her. But he had taken the marriage for granted and neglected it in the same way he was in danger of doing with our relationship.

The Blue Plate Special

Walk into a small-town café or roadside diner, and you're likely to see the daily blue plate special printed on a chalkboard above the cash register. For one low price, you get a main course—let's say, corned beef and cabbage—with maybe two side dishes of green beans and mashed potatoes, coffee or tea, and probably pudding or, if it's a really great place, homemade pie for dessert.

Always, under the description of that day's special, are the words "No Substitutions!" If you order the blue plate special, you agree to take the whole meal as described for the bargain price. You cannot substitute corn for the green beans, rice for the potatoes, cake for the pudding. I know you think the waiter or waitress should make an exception for you, but the good ones don't. You either take the blue plate special the way it comes on the menu, or you order something else.

Every relationship is like a blue plate special. When we fall in love, we go for the succulent corned beef, and we think, this is great. Corned beef is just what I want. And when we see a flaw or an imperfection, then we say, if only I could do something to change these green beans, everything would be perfect. I just don't like green beans. So we set out to cajole, plead, bribe—anything to get rid of the green beans.

The pitfall is that we spend so much time trying to change what can't be changed that we never get around to enjoying the main course. Instead of taking the green beans and leaving them on the plate while we enjoy the luscious corned beef, we keep trying to change the blue plate special to match our taste. We allow a great main course to grow cold and inedible while we whine like children about the vegetables we don't like.

Instead of enjoying intimacy and closeness with our spouses, we squander precious time and energy trying to get her to be more organized or him to be neater. Instead of deciding we can live with habitual lateness and delighting in a partner who adores us, we nag our way into divorce court. As far as I can tell, just as there are no substitutions on the blue plate special, there are no flawless partners. You don't get to change what you don't like on the blue plate special, and you don't get to change what you don't like in your partner.

I consider this one of our greatest sins in relationships. We so quickly take our partner's wonderful qualities for granted and then let those qualities deteriorate and go to waste by not appreciating them. Meanwhile, we spend countless hours, years, decades trying to change his or her modest imperfections, when what we should have been doing all along is admiring and basking in the glories of this magnificent person.

Spread the Good News

The bad news is, almost all of us do this. The good news is, it is easy to correct. Whatever gets our focus, gets our energy and power. If you focus on flaws, mistakes, and imperfections, then those weaknesses grow. On the other hand, if you focus on strengths and talents, then those qualities grow. I learned this principle when I first began training others to do what I had been doing successfully for some time, conducting time management seminars for corporations.

My first group of trainees had to stand in front of the group for twenty minutes at a time and practice leading a seminar while I observed and scribbled very astute and detailed notes—which, of course, consisted of all their mistakes. Afterward, I let them know what I had found wrong with their work so they could improve: "You didn't speak loudly enough. You didn't make the point clearly. You never answered Arnie's question."

After a few hours of work, however, instead of improving, my trainees could barely utter two sentences in front of the group. I was sure I had an inept bunch, but I asked a more experienced trainer to sit in on my session just to verify that I had a slow group. He identified the problem right away. And it wasn't with my trainees. He explained that because I was only pointing out flaws and mistakes, their inadequacies were getting more pronounced. "Everyone has weak points that need improvement," he said. "That's a given. However, if you work on their imperfections, they're not going to improve."

He encouraged me to use my perceptive and critical skills to bring about the opposite outcome. "Work on their strengths, and they will blossom," he said. "They'll never be perfect, but if you nurture their strong points, they will grow stronger. *Eventually, their strengths will overshadow their weaknesses.*"

In my next session, I made sure to tell the trainees the

things they did right. "It was great the way you got Joe's attention. You knew the material well, and your joke really broke the ice." The difference was remarkable: big improvements showed up right away. Once they achieved some confidence, and they trusted that I was their fan and wanted success for them, they readily began to fix the aspects of their work that needed correction. They were able to incorporate my suggestions for changes, and instead of shutting down, they started to improve and succeed.

The same is true with couples who have taken my course. When I ask them to describe what they fell in love with, they begin to open up, often after a long time of being shut down. Each person gets to listen to his or her spouse say things that have long gone unsaid and unremembered: "This was the best-looking man I had ever seen." "I knew she would always be honest; she oozed with integrity." "No one has ever made me laugh the way he did." "Her sense of adventure grabbed me—I knew life would never be boring."

As each spouse opens up and drinks in the love and attraction, he or she becomes more appealing and full of fun and passion right before our eyes. "Oldyweds" who had actually forgotten these feelings ever existed rediscover them. When they express them to each other as they did when they first fell in love, they become alive and vibrant again.

I don't mean to say that problems don't exist and don't need some attention. We will handle those "how-tos" in later chapters. But as with the example of my seminar leader trainees, when you have a solid foundation of expressed love, adoration, devotion, and appreciation, problem solving and correction come much more naturally and easily. Use your attention to empower what is working, what is wonderful about your partner.

about the author

NITA TUCKER has been presenting her popular seminars on "How Not to Stay Single" to sold-out audiences in cities across the United States for years. *How Not to Stay Single After 40* will finally apply her amazingly successful formula for finding a romantic relationship to this group of singles who have been overlooked until now. She often appears on radio and television, including *The Today Show* and *Oprah*. She lives in Santa Fe.

Whether you're looking for a loving, committed relationship or are hoping to make one last, Nita Tucker outlines the action steps you should take to move from merely wishing to really doing. Tucker is also the author of:

How Not to Stay Single
0-517-88637-5.
$12.00 paperback
(Canada: $15.00)

How Not to Screw It Up
0-609-80333-6.
$12.00 paperback
(Canada: $15.00)

THREE RIVERS PRESS • NEW YORK
Available from Three Rivers Press
wherever books are sold.

NOTES

NOTES